TEACHING THE MENTALLY RETARDED CHILD

TEACHING THE MENTALLY
RETARDED CHILD a family care approach

Kathryn E. Barnard, R.N., B.S.N., M.S.N., Ph.D.

Professor of Nursing, University of Washington School of Nursing, and associated with Child Development and Mental Retardation Center, University of Washington, Seattle, Washington

Marcene L. Powell, R.N., B.S.N., M.N.

Assistant Professor, University of Washington School of Nursing, and associated with Child Development and Mental Retardation Center, University of Washington, Seattle, Washington

THE C. V. MOSBY COMPANY

Saint Louis 1972

To those who have inspired us

our parents
    professors
    colleagues
    students
    children and their families

PREFACE

Handicapped children and their families present problems that demand attention, study, and creative solution by members of the helping professions. Many of the problems of these children and families involve daily living functions that relate to nurturing, caring, and teaching.

We have found that the principles and techniques used to alleviate the problems of the mentally retarded and their families are widely applicable to many other handicapping conditions. This book is directed to the care of the handicapped child in infancy and early preschool years who lives with his family. This period is critical in relation to the child's development of skills and independence. It also is an important time for promoting the healthy adjustment of the parents and other family members to the problems of a handicapped child.

In working with practitioners from the various health disciplines who are helping the families of mentally retarded children with problems of daily care and management, we have sensed their desire to add to their knowledge of human growth and development in order to apply it to the developmental problems of retarded children. Health care professionals as well as parents are today vitally concerned with improving the environmental conditions that influence development, management, and the training needs of these children.

This book presents the information, the rationale, and the process we used to work with handicapped children and their families. We appreciate what these children and parents have taught us. We now have hope and confidence that the problems can be dealt with more effectively, to the mutual benefit of the parents, other family members, and the handicapped child. For this reason we are committed to presenting this material, which we anticipate will broaden and strengthen the efforts of others who are involved in this area of health care.

Kathryn E. Barnard
Marcene L. Powell

CONTENTS

section one
NURSING AND THE HANDICAPPED CHILD

1
The nursing responsibility

PREVENTION

Nursing has a primary responsibility in several major areas within the field of mental retardation and handicapping conditions in childhood. One principal task is prevention of handicapping conditions, not only through counteracting the conditions that cause these handicaps, but also through circumventing the secondary retardation or handicaps that result from improper management.

In the area of primary prevention, nurses have responsibility in programs of nutrition, immunization, and environmental modification. It is vital that children, teen-agers, and adults maintain an adequate dietary pattern, particularly in relation to protein and calories. The mother's general health and nutrition before, as well as during, her pregnancy are significant factors influencing fetal growth and development.[1]

The nurse becomes a primary source of nutritional information and guidance for families she sees in the community, clinic, and hospital. It is important for the nurse to obtain dietary histories of the children and entire family. The nurse's interpretation of the results of a daily diet record kept by the mother can be the basis for conversations about nutrition and metabolism in growth and development. The record, viewed with other information, might reveal the need for reductions in feedings in an inactive child, increased feedings in a hyperactive child, dietary supplements, closer monitoring of height and weight records, or changes in feeding practices such as helping a mother and child make the transition to different textured foods.

The nurse should take liberal advantage of the availability of state and local nutritionists to gain information she can use for families. Nurses must motivate the people they see toward an automatic pattern of adequate nutrition and, further, assume more responsibility to see that those who do not have adequate food get it.

The disabling conditions that can result from childhood infections cannot be understated, especially for children in overcrowded conditions in which food is inadequate and sanitation is poor. Levels of immunization for diseases such as poliomyelitis, pertussis, and measles are far below a desirable goal. Almost half the under-19 population of the United States have not been adequately immunized against diphtheria-pertussis-tetanus.[2]

Nurses must assume more responsibility for health teaching if they are to change the picture of disability. Parents need to be taught and consistently reinforced for carrying out preventive health practices. In addition to nutrition and immunization, it is important for the nurse to teach concepts of early environmental stimulation. Early environmental stimulation consists of rearranging circumstances in the environment that reinforce a child's strengths and skills. It puts into action the principles of capitalizing on readiness to learn new tasks and skills. A systematic intervention program can reduce a child's deficits in adaptive behaviors, self-help skills, socialization, and language.

CASE FINDING

The second major nursing responsibility is case finding, an area in which nurses have been involved for many years. The public health nurse in the community is in a strategic position; proximity often enables her to discover developmental problems of young children that otherwise might go undetected until school age. Concepts presented in *A Developmental Approach to Case Finding,*[3] *The Denver Developmental Screening Test,*[4] and the *Washington Guide to Promoting Development in the Young Child* (Chapter 5) have prompted nurses to engage in even more systematic assessment and case finding in child development.

A few facts help illustrate the magnitude of the problem of case finding. In 1970 it was estimated that between 100,000 and 200,000 babies who are mentally retarded are born each year. The causes of mental retardation can be identified in approximately one fourth of the cases. In the remaining cases, inadequacies in prenatal and perinatal health care, nutrition, child rearing, and social and environmental opportunities are suspected as causes of retardation. As of 1970 more than 6 million persons in the United States were mentally retarded. Of these, 2.5 million were under the age of 20. As commonly defined, the mentally retarded population can be divided into those who are educable, those who are trainable, and those who are unable to care for themselves. It is estimated that of the individuals under 20 years of age who are mentally retarded, 75% are mildly retarded, or educable, 15% are moderately retarded, or trainable, 8% are severely retarded, and 2% are profoundly retarded and unable to care for themselves.[5]

Birth defects are also a major cause of death and disability in the United States. Congenital abnormalities and defects contibute to 500,000 fetal deaths each year and affect the daily lives of 15 million persons of all ages. During 1963 to 1965 it was estimated that one in twelve children 6 to 11 years of age in the United States had a speech defect and one in nine had defective vision. During the 1960's the incidence of blindness in persons under 20 years of age was 45,000, with approximately 5,000 new cases each year.[5]

SERIAL OBSERVATIONS

A significant concept being integrated into early case finding is that health care professionals no longer wait for a full-blown syndrome to manifest itself but operate increasingly on the basis of suspicion. This means that there is greater emphasis placed on the importance of making serial and sequential observations on an infant or child who is not following normal patterns of development before a specific diagnosis is made. Nurses recognize too that screening for handicaps does not begin and end with one assessment procedure. It requires that children be observed at repeated intervals. Early case finding can be started with the newborn infant in the first 24-hour period. The practice of early hospital discharge for maternity and pediatric patients dictates responsibility for continuity of care to the nurse in the hospital and the nurse in the community. Nurses are examining infants in a more in-depth way by assuming responsibility for eliciting the early neurological reflexes such as the Moro, plantar, palmar, stepping, sucking, and rooting reflexes. At the same time they are doing surface appraisals, that is, looking for symmetry of structure and function and the presence of one or more minor anomalies that could signal the need to be alert for a major defect in an infant.

Nurses are alert to the necessity for accurate measurements during this newborn period and obtain head, chest, height, and weight records early. These become base line measurements if later interventions are necessary. Nurses are in a strategic position for early referral, anticipatory guidance, early counseling of parents, and early activation of infant stimulation programs. It is through the application of knowledge about the normal child that nurses feel more secure in assuming the responsibilities for independent judgment in working with mentally retarded children. Some of the most characteristic delays in development that children with retardation display are (1) not sitting up by 8 months of age, (2) not walking by 15 to 18 months of age, (3) not responding to verbal commands, and (4) not using expressive language.

The largest number of children with developmental delays are brought to professional attention at 4 to 5 years of age, since they may have their development assessed in a comprehensive manner for the first time at this age for school entrance. A considerable percentage of cases are picked up at 7 to 10 years of age when the child is increasingly required to use symbolic language. At this period, learning takes place on a less concrete, more abstract level. A child in school who is not performing academically or who is presenting a behavior problem should be referred to an appropriate resource for study.

PHYSICAL CHARACTERISTICS

In addition to developmental assessment, it is important to observe physical characteristics carefully. The following guide presents a systematic method of surface inspection of the newborn. In each category a listing of questionable variations appears. This listing can be used as a reference in case finding;

OBSERVATIONAL GUIDE TO ASSESS
THE NEWBORN[6,7]

Name _____

Age _____

Physical characteristics observed	Surface inspection to gain clinical data	Selected common variations in structure or function that can be indices to suspicion
1. General appearance	Postural attitudes, muscle tone, activity levels, state of comfort, responsiveness	Hypotonicity Marked hypertonicity Marked inactivity or hyperactivity Asymmetry of body parts
2. Skin	Color, degree, uniformity, degrees of cyanosis or pallor (generalized or peripheral) Eruptions Hydration Hemorrhagic manifestations Rash, inflammation Pigmentation, nevi, subcutaneous nodules, desquamation Presence, absence, and degree of jaundice Striae, wrinkling, vernix caseosa Texture Turgor Elasticity Lanugo (quantity and distribution) Sensitivity Temperature Parchment Opacity Edema	Café au lait spots Raised capillary hemangiomas elsewhere than face or posterior of neck Pigmented nevi Low hairline posteriorly Sparse or spotty hair Mongoloid spots (in Caucasians)
3. Head	Size, shape, circumference, control and movement, sutures, forcep marks, moulding	Flat occiput Prominent occiput
a. Skull	Contours, symmetry, moulding, resistance of skull bones to gentle pressure	Microcephaly } Requires Macrocephaly } measurement
b. Scalp	Presence, quantity, texture, and distribution of hair and location of hairline	Hirsutism

Physical characteristics observed	Surface inspection to gain clinical data	Selected common variations in structure or function that can be indices to suspicion
3. Head—cont'd		
c. Fontanels. anterior, posterior	Cephalhematoma, subcutaneous nodules around occiput Tension, size (cm.), pulsations Closure and number	Large posterior fontanel Large anterior fontanel Bulging or depressed fontanels Premature or late closure of fontanels
4. Face	Shape and symmetry of parts, distance between mouth and nose, depth of nasolabial fold, distribution of hair, size of mandible, fullness of cheeks, facial movements when resting and crying to evaluate integrity of innervation of facial musculature	Defect in bony orbits of face Protruding forehead Absent ramus of mandible
5. Eyes	Placement, symmetry, distance between inner canthi, lacrimation, clarity and luster of corneas, pupillary reaction, opacity of lenses, placement of eyebrows, lids, distribution of eyelashes, color of iris, muscular control, position of pupils in relationship to palpebral fissures	Absent eyelashes or eyebrows Eyebrows extending to midline Cataracts Corneal opacity Bilateral inner epicanthal folds Severe upward or downward slant of palpebral fissures (eye sockets) Eyes set close together or far apart Size of eyes Sparse eyebrows or lashes Speckled iris Ptosis of eyelid
6. Nose	Exterior appearance, shape, patency, discharge, placement in relationship to eyes and mouth, symmetry, septum	Low or flat nasal bridge Small nares, large nares, inability to breathe through nares Beaklike nose

OBSERVATIONAL GUIDE TO ASSESS THE NEWBORN—CONT'D

Physical characteristics observed	Surface inspection to gain clinical data	Selected common variations in structure or function that can be indices to suspicion
7. Ears	Placement, form, position, and size of pinna, symmetry, firmness	High or low placement Lack of usual fold of helix Periauricular or auricular skin tags Small ears (asymmetrical size) Severe slant of ears
8. Mouth	Size, shape, placement, symmetry, color, mucosa, anterior mouth cavity, pharynx, lip margins	Cleft lip—lip fistulas Cleft palate Small mouth
9. Tongue	Size, mobility, color, coating, grooves	Protruding tongue—incomplete lip closure Short tongue Uncoordinated movements
10. Chin	Size	
11. Neck	Size, position, movement, contour, flexion	Extra creases or folds Short neck Webbing
12. Thorax	Shape, symmetry, retractions and pulsations, size, position, and distance between nipples, length of sternum, palpation of breast tissue, respiratory activity, depth and rate, chest circumference	High-placed nipples Wide-spaced nipples Prominent or depressed sternum Asymmetrical movement of thorax Short thoracic cage
13. Abdomen and navel	Size and contour, respiratory movements, musculature, tension, pulsations, presence of umbilical vein, two umbilical arteries, surface of umbilicus	Umbilical hernia Inguinal hernias Palpable masses
14. Genitalia	Male: circumcision, meatal opening, foreskin, surface and size of scrotum, position of testis in scrotum Female: size of labia, secretions, edema of genitals	Hypospadias Hypoplasia of labia majora

Physical characteristics observed	Surface inspection to gain clinical data	Selected common variations in structure or function that can be indices to suspicion
15. Rectum	Patency	Deep sacral dimple Imperforate anus
16. Hips	Posture, motion, movement, flexion, and symmetry	Dislocation of hip
17. Extremities, hand, feet	Range of motion, movement, length, symmetry, posture, tremors, number of digits, flexion, creases of hands, quality of nails, resistance to passive movement	Absence of nails Complete simian crease Unusual crease patterns Clinodactyly or polydactyly Short hands—incurved fifth finger Asymmetrical length of digits Joint hypermobility Joint limitation
18. Joints and spine	Posture, symmetry, mobility, alignment	Protrusions of spinal cord Depressed areas
19. Cry	Tone, pitch, frequency, duration, intensity, alternate periods of excitability and quietness, lacrimation	High-pitched, shrill cry Low, coarse cry

however, it would be important to note any other characteristic that appears unusual from a number of observations made of the infant. The presence of any of these variations, appearing singly or in combination with another, requires additional assessment by the physician.

EARLY PROGRAMING

Comprehensive auditory, motor, sensory, and language stimulation programs have been created for infants and children with deficits in these areas. A suggested infant stimulation model that could be used to enrich an infant's environment and promote his subsequent development is summarized as follows.[8]

SUGGESTED EARLY INFANT STIMULATION MODEL

1. Hold the infant and provide tactile stimulation (touch, rub, pat, kiss, bounce).

2. Talk to the infant and play with him as you bathe, feed, and dress him.

3. Encourage movement by exercise of the infant's arms and legs when he is bathed and dressed.

4. Dress the infant in clothes that do not bind to allow him freedom to move his arms and legs.

5. Provide the infant with changes in his environment, such as changing the position of his crib in the room and putting him in different positions in the crib.

6. Place the infant in different rooms during the day.

7. Place the infant at different heights (on the floor, on the sofa or chair, in the crib).

8. Place the infant on surfaces having varied textures (smooth, rough, cool, dry, wet, cotton, terrycloth, satin, fur, velvet, etc.).

9. Place objects of various sizes and textures in the crib or within the infant's reach.

10. Alternate the toys frequently instead of giving the infant everything at one time.

11. Feed the infant from alternate sides.

12. Avoid leaving the infant or child unattended for prolonged periods of time.

13. Make special efforts to attend to the infant when he is quiet and amusing himself.

14. Practice consistency in approaches to the infant.[8]

MANAGEMENT

The third major task the nurse has in mental retardation is that of management. Nurses have become increasingly developmentally oriented and, as a result, have become skillful in working with children who are suspected of developmental deviations or who have been diagnosed as mentally retarded. Persons who help retarded children achieve independence and autonomy should recognize the necessity of utilizing principles of developmental psychology and education.

Parents profit from support on a continuing, ongoing basis to help them express how they feel, work through their feelings, and be supported in their feelings of adequacy in their roles as parents. Nurses can be instrumental in assessing family interpersonal functioning on a periodic and objective basis.

Using developmental base line information, nurses can help parents gain a concept of their child's developmental level. Periodic assessments of a child's developmental milestones are important in determining the child's level of functioning and helping parents determine cooperatively his readiness for new skills.

Literature such as *David*[9] and *The World of Nigel Hunt*[10] is oriented toward helping parents gain more understanding of children who are mentally retarded and can be referred to parents for their personal reading. Often parents can gain additional support and knowledge from involvement in a group of parents who have children with handicaps.

Parents need to be guided in the realization that short-term goals for their child's achievement will ultimately help them achieve the optimal or long-range goal for his development. Specific assistance can be directed toward stressing the importance of repetition when a child is learning a new skill. The nurse can provide anticipatory guidance regarding limit setting, as well as suggestions for varied stimulation for the individual child.

The concept of looking at positive strengths and assets of children and families rather than just detecting abnormal or negative features is used. This allows one to capitalize on new capacities as they emerge and build on strengths that already exist.

Nurses are helping parents manage common problems of feeding, dressing, toileting, and providing socializing experiences for their children; they are providing creative and innovative applications of techniques to aid growth and development in early environmental stimulation programs.

REFERENCES

1. Committee on Maternal Nutrition, Food and Nutrition Board, National Research Council: Maternal nutrition and the course of pregnancy, Washington, D. C., 1970, National Academy of Sciences.
2. White House Conference on Children: Report to the President, Washington, D. C., 1970, Superintendent of Documents, U. S. Government Printing Office.
3. Haynes, U.: A developmental approach to case finding, Children's Bureau Publication No. 2017-1969, Washington, D. C., Superintendent of Documents, U. S. Government Printing Office.
4. Frankenberg, W. K., and Dodds, J. B.: The Denver Developmental Screening Test, J. Pediat. 71:181-191, 1967.
5. White House Conference on Children: Profiles of children, Washington, D. C., 1970, Superintendent of Documents, U. S. Government Printing Office.
6. Smith, D. W.: Recognizable patterns of human malformation, Philadelphia, 1970, W. B. Saunders Co.
7. Marden, P. M., Smith, D. W., and McDonald, M. J.: Congenital anomalies in the newborn infant, including minor variations, J. Pediat. 64:357-371, 1964.
8. Bell, B.: Nursing 600 project, independent study, Seattle, 1970, University of Washington. (Unpublished.)
9. Roberts, R., and Roberts, B.: David, Richmond, Va., 1968, John Knox Press.
10. The world of Nigel Hunt: the diary of a mongoloid youth, New York, 1967, Garrett Publications.

ADDITIONAL READINGS

Frankenberg, W. K., and Dodds, J. B.: Denver Developmental Screening Test, Denver, 1967, Ladoca Project and Publishing Foundation.
Gellis, S. S., and Feingold, M.: Atlas of mental retardation syndromes. Visual diagnosis of

facies and physical findings, Washington, D. C., 1968, U. S. Department of Health, Education, and Welfare, Division of Mental Retardation.

Ingram, T. T. S.: The new approach to early diagnosis of handicaps in childhood, Develop. Med. Child Neurol. **11:**270-290, 1969.

Knobloch, H., and Pasamanick, B.: The developmental behavioral approach to the neurologic examination in infancy, Child Develop. **33:**181-192, 1962.

Koch, R., Graliker, B., Bronston, W., et al.: Mental retardation in early childhood, Amer. J. Dis. Child. **109:**243-251, 1965.

Lesser, A. J.: Accent on prevention through improved service, Children **11:**13-18, Jan.-Feb., 1964.

Murphy, L. B.: Appendix A: The vulnerability inventory. In Dittmann, L. L., editor: Early child care, New York, 1968, Atherton Press.

Murphy, L. B.: Assessments of infants and young children. In Dittmann, L. L., editor: Early child care, New York, 1968, Atherton Press.

Reaser, G. P.: Identification of infants and young children with high risk for mental retardation and some approaches to early intervention. (Paper presented at Fourth National Workshop for Nurses in Mental Retardation, Miami, Florida, April 6, 1967.) In Nursing in mental retardation programs, Washington, D. C., 1967, Children's Bureau, Department of Health, Education, and Welfare.

Scrimshaw, N. S.: Infant malnutrition and adult learning, Saturday Review **52:**11, March 16, 1969.

Shapiro, S.: Relationship of selected prenatal factors to pregnancy outcome and congenital anomalies, Amer. J. Public Health **55:**268-282, 1965.

Winick, M., and Rosso, P.: The effect of severe early malnutrition on cellular growth of human brain, Pediat. Res. **3:**181, 1969.

2
Concepts related to child development, handicapping conditions, and nursing

The concepts that provide the framework for effective nursing in child development and handicapping conditions are as follows:

1. Development is influenced by genetic and environmental factors.

2. The human being is an organized system capable of organizing.

3. Play, imitative behavior, and language are the means by which the child enters the world of others.

4. Development proceeds in an orderly sequence that is largely determined by maturation, not by learning.

5. Self-care skills are complex sequences of many behaviors that are integrated toward functional purposes.

6. Learning is indicated by a change in behavior not accounted for by maturation alone; it is facilitated by reinforcement of that behavior.

7. Each child maintains a pattern of physical, intellectual, and psychological growth; a disruption in the pattern, either a delay or an acceleration, should be carefully observed.

8. The child's development occurs within the framework of the family.

9. Mental retardation and other handicapping conditions present complex medical, psychological, and sociological problems.

10. The nursing process is directed toward assisting the family with a retarded or handicapped child in developing and maintaining as much independent functioning of their child as possible.

Each of these concepts will be discussed and some examples given of how they apply to the nursing rationale and action in working with the mentally retarded child and his family.

DEVELOPMENT IS INFLUENCED BY GENETIC AND ENVIRONMENTAL FACTORS

The individual's potential for growth and development is limited by his genetic makeup. Environment, however, influences the individual's ability and rate in achieving his capacity for growth and development. Even at birth a child's potential for development has already come under the influence of environment in the form of intrauterine factors such as maternal nutrition. After birth the child is affected by countless aspects of the environment, including parental care, chemical and biological agents, physical surroundings, and socioeconomic factors. Retardation may be caused by genetic or environmental factors or a combination of factors. The majority of cases of retardation are thought to result from unfavorable environmental conditions, including inadequate prenatal care and various forms of social and psychological deprivation. Illustrations can be found, from height and intelligence measurements, of how environmental factors are related to variations in an individual's development. Differences in height are likely to be related to (1) quality and quantity of nutrition provided by the environment and utilization of the appropriate nutritional elements by the individual and (2) sanitation, disease prevention, and the availability and utilization of medical care when needed in regard to general intellectual levels.

The differences in levels of intelligence are thought to be related to (1) stimulation provided in the environment for conceptual development, (2) the extent to which affection and rewards are related to verbal reasoning accomplishments, and (3) encouragement of active interaction with problems, exploration of the environment, and learning of new skills.

There are periods in which growth and development are rapid and periods in which growth is slow or in which there is little perceptible change. Up until 5 years of age there is a period of rapid growth for all body systems during which behavior patterns are formed and stabilized. It is during this period of rapid change or growth that the environment input makes the most difference.[1]

THE HUMAN BEING IS AN ORGANIZED SYSTEM CAPABLE OF ORGANIZING

As the nervous system matures, the child has an increasing capacity not only to take in auditory, visual, and tactile stimuli but also to make meaningful associations from what he takes in. Increasingly, he develops the ability to sort out the stimuli that are important in making associations and ignore those that are not.

The mentally retarded child seems to have more difficulty than others do in taking in stimuli, sorting them, and reacting appropriately. In order to learn, it is of the utmost importance that he have cues in his environment to help him know what to do and that his appropriate behavior be reinforced. He has a better chance for learning if his habit of paying attention to distinct stimuli is developed and practiced.

The following is an example of a learning situation—learning how to button a shirt—and how it might be organized:

Process	Problem	Solution
Taking in stimuli	Not knowing what is important to task	Orienting child's eyes and hands to button and buttonhole
Reacting appropriately	Not knowing what action is required	Providing direction of what to do with his hands, showing him, praising his accomplishments
Attending	Not applying his sensory capacities to task	Keeping his eyes and hands focused on task

PLAY, IMITATIVE BEHAVIOR, AND LANGUAGE ARE THE MEANS BY WHICH THE CHILD ENTERS THE WORLD OF OTHERS

The infant's play with his own arms, hands, and feet is the beginning of his efforts to explore the environment. Through play with others and with objects, the child learns to experience his world and has repeated opportunities to feel, hear, and see things he must come to understand and to master. The process of play is not automatic; it can be developed in stages. He must be taught to be aware of things in the environment and encouraged to feel, see, and hear them.

The child masters many early learning tasks through imitation; hence the adult may not be consciously aware of teaching them. The game of patty-cake teaches something about rhythm, motion, and body coordination. The child takes in the action and, gradually, with many repetitions, learns to imitate the behavior; only later does he perceive the idea behind the action and language. Imitative behavior can be instituted readily by sensorimotor stimulation through the use of many toys and simple repetitive games. In the retarded child, imitation may not develop as rapidly as in the normal child; hence more concentrated effort is required to set the stage for its occurrence.

The lack of language development in retarded individuals is commonly perceived. Many parents say, "If he could just talk, he would be normal." The lack of language development is one of the factors in the gap between the retarded child and normal children in his age group, which increases as he grows older. Basic language patterns begin as the infant coos and babbles and the parent repeats back. After the first several months, we see a reversal, with the parent setting up the speech model for the child to imitate. One cannot stress enough the importance of feedback in the learning-responding situation. The retarded child should have an appropriate language-rich environment. The sounds he makes and his attempts at speech should be highly reinforced. Lack of feedback to low initial speech output may well contribute to the slowness of language development in retarded individuals.

The child who does not develop play and imitative behavior or language has no alternative but to remain in his own world. In fact, this frequently happens among institutionalized retardates, who manifest a great deal of self-stimulatory behavior, that is, self-abuse. They have developed no mechanisms for relating to others.

DEVELOPMENT PROCEEDS IN AN ORDERLY SEQUENCE THAT IS LARGELY DETERMINED BY MATURATION, NOT BY LEARNING

Development occurs in a cephalocaudal direction and proceeds from the gross to the more specific muscle masses. The infant develops head control before trunk and extremity control. Posture develops first, then function. This orderly sequence and direction in development must be considered when teaching, for example, a child to walk. It is essential to start developing first those behaviors that lead up to walking—head control, extremity control, and equilibrium responses in sitting, kneeling, and standing. As the muscles are used, they both grow and develop. The following table from Jensen[2] represents the range of normal development of certain basic developmental landmarks.

Estimated ranges of normal for developmental landmarks*

Developmental landmarks	Range of normal	Mean or norm
Symmetrical posturing predominates	2-6 mo.	4 mo.
Smiles at stimulation	1-4 mo.	6 wk.
Laughs out loud	2-6 mo.	4 mo.
Turns head to the bell	3-7 mo.	5 mo.
Rolls from supine to prone position	3-9 mo.	5½ mo.
Sits alone steadily	5-11 mo.	8 mo.
Transfers toy from hand to hand	5-9 mo.	7 mo.
Neat pincer grasp (grasps the pellet)	7-13 mo.	11 mo.
Walks alone	7-18 mo.	13 mo.
Vocabulary of two words (besides ma-ma and da-da)	9-26 mo.	12 mo.

*From Jensen, G. D.: The well child's problems: management in the first six years, Chicago, 1962, Year Book Medical Publishers, Inc., p. 25. Used with permission.

SELF-CARE SKILLS ARE COMPLEX SEQUENCES OF MANY BEHAVIORS THAT ARE INTEGRATED TOWARD FUNCTIONAL PURPOSES

A self-care skill allows the individual to operate within his environment to meet his needs—eating, for example. Although it seems rather simple to us at first, when the task is broken down, we become aware of the sequence of complex behaviors that goes into the function. The child must pay attention to the feeding situation. He must be able to pick up the spoon, bring it to his mouth, swallow the food, and then return the spoon to the bowl or plate. The integration of behavior sequences involves eye-hand coordination and judgment of spatial relationships.

The nurse will be concerned with determining the self-care skills that the child has already acquired and those he needs help in developing. She must then analyze the individual tasks that make up the skill, for it is through mastering one step at a time that the retarded child will learn.

LEARNING IS INDICATED BY A CHANGE IN BEHAVIOR NOT ACCOUNTED FOR BY MATURATION ALONE; IT IS FACILITATED BY REINFORCEMENT OF THAT BEHAVIOR

In promoting the learning process, it is useful to keep in mind the following basic principles:

Principle	Example
Learning is an active process; child learns by doing	Child learns that things go into containers by putting them in
Learning proceeds from simple to complex	Child learns to take things apart before he learns to put them together
Learning is enhanced by maturational readiness	Child is more capable of learning to control bladder elimination after he can hold urine and after he associates feeling of fullness with voluntary release of sphincter
Learning is enhanced by meaningful practice	When child is learning to feed himself with a spoon, he needs many opportunities to handle spoon and should be repeatedly guided in correct movement for scooping and bowl-to-mouth delivery
Organization promotes retention and application of learning	Child is helped in learning to dress himself if his clothes are always in same place and same sequence of actions is followed each time
Positive consequences increase likelihood that a behavior will be repeated	If child likes to have mother's attention and mother makes a pleasant fuss over him when he puts his toys away, he is likely to do it again
Negative or neutral consequences decrease likelihood that a behavior will be repeated	If child makes sounds and parents ignore him, he may gradually decrease behavior
Imitation of others' behavior promotes learning	If child observes a playmate putting a ring on a peg, he is likely to do the same without verbal instruction

EACH CHILD MAINTAINS A PATTERN OF PHYSICAL, INTELLECTUAL, AND PSYCHOLOGICAL GROWTH; A DISRUPTION IN THE PATTERN, EITHER A DELAY OR AN ACCELERATION, SHOULD BE CAREFULLY OBSERVED

There are several indices of physical growth available. The Wetzel Grid, the Stuart Growth Grid, and the Iowa Growth Chart are examples of guides that nurses have used. Charts are available also on growth of head circumference.[3] Variations in the child's own growth pattern are important to note so that intervention can be provided when necessary. A discussion of growth charts is available in most pediatric medical textbooks.[4]

Nurses today are becoming more familiar with those motor, imitative, attending, and problem-solving behaviors that serve as indicators of cognitive growth. It is important that the nurse contribute valid observations that will aid those responsible for evaluation, diagnosis, and prediction about the child's later abilities.

Serial observations are essential in providing the information necessary to determine the child's pattern of development. Particularly with the young child, it is important to have periodic measurements before instituting a program of intervention.

THE CHILD'S DEVELOPMENT OCCURS WITHIN THE FRAMEWORK OF THE FAMILY

The fact of having a retarded child provokes certain emotional responses in family members that affect their child-rearing practices. The initial reaction to having a retarded child may be a combination of shock and denial of the child's handicap. This is a defense mechanism that allows parents to cope with the situation. While in this stage, they are immobilized in terms of planning or dealing effectively with problems the child may have. The task at this time is to help the parents become aware of their child's handicap whether or not they are specifically told about it. It is questionable whether diagnostic evaluations as such are of benefit to parents at this time unless they are helped to acquire awareness of the handicap. The next stage is one of frustration when many questions of why the retardation happened and what it will mean constantly confront the parents. Parents may be overprotective in caring and planning for their child.

During these initial parental reactions the nurse provides emotional support to the parents and helps them make a realistic appraisal of the child's strengths, as well as his weaknesses. One of the most important objectives in dealing with parents of mentally retarded children is to increase their feelings of adequacy as individuals and as parents. One means of doing this is to help them know how to respond to a child whose development and behavior differ from the normal.

As parents develop more objectivity, they become more capable of effectively involving themselves in plans to increase the child's level of functioning. Parents must be a part of any planning to work with a child. The care and rearing of the child are their responsibilities. Guidance by others should be directed toward helping them become more effective parents. Any program to work with the child must consider the total family's needs and proceed within that framework.

It should be recognized that the parents' physical and mental conditions, personalities, and marital problems and other demands placed on them affect their involvement in working with the child. The nurse may be able to help them overcome barriers through referral to social service agencies, clinics, physicians, etc., as well as through her own efforts. In planning with the parents, the nurse must keep in mind their individual qualities, situations, and limitations, not only for the sake of realistic planning, but also because each parent needs recognition and understanding as a person in his or her own right and not merely as the parent of a retarded child.

MENTAL RETARDATION AND OTHER HANDICAPPING CONDITIONS PRESENT COMPLEX MEDICAL, PSYCHOLOGICAL, AND SOCIAL PROBLEMS

An interdisciplinary approach provides the framework for comprehensive services. Several interdisciplinary models are commonly used. One is the medical model. This is generally seen in the diagnostic or clinical setting, where emphasis is on evaluation of suspected retardation. Another model is the psychiatric or mental health model, which is based on approaching mental retardation as a problem of adaptation, with the emphasis on family coping patterns. The third model is the educational model. One of the major problems of the retarded child, as we have previously stated, is learning. Nurses and those in disciplines other than education are becoming more involved in the educational model in approaching the problem.

One exciting, as well as frustrating, aspect about an interdisciplinary approach is that roles change as the team composition alters. Although a person's professional background provides a basic orientation, there should be flexibility to do that which one is best prepared for and most capable of doing. With a particular family, this might mean that the nurse takes on the interpretation of findings to the family in view of her relationship and ease of communication. With another family, the nurse might advise the social worker or psychologist about aspects of home management so that they may include this information in their work with the family.

To appreciate the team concept, watch a basketball team in action. There is a great deal of supportive teamwork that leads up to the end goal—making the basket. Although several members of the team contribute toward setting up the conditions, generally only one player gets the ball into the basket. This is directly applicable to an interdisciplinary team. The members must work collaboratively toward the same goal; this involves sharing knowledge and abilities.

The spectrum of professionals concerned with the retarded includes physicians, nurses, psychologists, social workers, speech and hearing pathologists, nutritionists, neurologists, psychiatrists, dentists, educators, physical therapists, occupational therapists, and recreational therapists. Although every professional skill is not essential in every case, it is from the selection and integration of all appropriate ones that effective planning and implementation proceed.

If the nurse is operating without benefit of a interdisciplinary approach, she might look into the prospect of creating one or more approximation of one. For example, it may be within her responsibility to identify potential resources in the community for a family and to coordinate their services to the family. She can be alert to the clues that a child needs further neurological assessment or the services of an ophthalmologist.

THE NURSING PROCESS IS DIRECTED TOWARD ASSISTING THE FAMILY WITH A RETARDED OR HANDICAPPED CHILD IN DEVELOPING AND MAINTAINING AS MUCH INDEPENDENT FUNCTIONING OF THEIR CHILD AS POSSIBLE

First, the nursing process involves determining what the problems are in the child's development and the family's adaptation, then devising a strategy to deal with them.

Nursing involves a process that results in change. In the field of mental retardation this process is directed toward assisting the parents and promoting and maintaining independent functioning in the child with developmental delays or deficits. The nurse needs to develop a systematic approach to planning interventions in the care of the young retarded child. This approach includes the following steps:

1. Clarification of the nurse's role and establishment of rapport
2. Identification of parental concerns
3. Identification of family patterns of interaction and value systems
4. Observation of the child in his environment
5. Assessment of the functional level of the child's development
6. Analysis of observations
7. Identification of behavior of the child and family that should be strengthened or otherwise altered
8. Task analysis of the self-care skills to be taught
9. Structuring the learning situation
10. Evaluation of the method and progress made

The challenging aspects of the nursing process with the mentally retarded child and his family are derived from the changes that can be generated in development of self-help skills or implementation of behavioral change. The ability to promote changes is largely dependent on an increased sensitivity to an objective interpretation of behaviors and a problem-solving approach. The ultimate goal in this nursing process is to rearrange the learning environment to generate more independent behaviors of the child with developmental deficits. *In assisting families in the care of their children, the nursing process begins with the first contact with the family.*

REFERENCES

1. Bloom, B. S.: Stability and change in human characteristics, New York, 1964, John Wiley & Sons, Inc.
2. Jensen, G. D.: The well child's problems: management in the first six years, Chicago, 1962, Year Book Medical Publishers, Inc.
3. Nelson, G.: Head circumference from birth to eighteen years, practical composite international and interracial graphs, Pediatrics 41:106-114, 1968.
4. Whipple, D.: Dynamics of development: euthenic pediatrics, New York, 1966, McGraw-Hill Book Co.

ADDITIONAL READINGS

Barnard, K., editor: Symposium on mental retardation, Nursing Clinics of North America, Philadelphia, December, 1966, W. B. Saunders Co.

Falkner, F.: Human development, Philadelphia, 1966, W. B. Saunders Co.

Hunt, J. M.: Intelligence and experience, New York, 1961, The Ronald Press.

Hunt, J. M.: How children develop intellectually, Children 11:83-91, May-June, 1964.

Maier, H. W.: Three theories of child development, New York, 1965, Harper & Row, Publishers.

Nursing in mental retardation programs, Proceedings of the Fourth Annual Workshop, University of Miami, April 4 to 7, 1967, sponsored by Children's Bureau, U. S. Department of Health, Education, and Welfare and Child Development Center (out of print).

Philips, I., editor: Prevention and treatment of mental retardation, New York, 1966, Basic Books.

Read, M. S.: Malnutrition and learning, Bethesda, Md., 1969, Information Office, National Institute of Child Health and Human Development, National Institutes of Health.

section two
FAMILY CONSIDERATIONS

3

How families react to the crisis of having a handicapped child

An important aspect of dealing with handicapping conditions such as mental retardation relates to working with the family of the child who is handicapped. The parents and siblings experience certain emotional states as a reaction to having a child with developmental deviations in their family. A fairly predictable pattern seems to exist that the family, particularly the parents, go through in handling the problems that the retarded child presents. It seems logical to assume that having a deviant child presents a threat to the parents' marital integration and the family's continuity. This threat might best be handled with development of a plan in which the family decide what their goals for the child are and how they might achieve them. This chapter will discuss how families react to the crisis of having a deviant child and how persons in nursing can be of assistance. The influences that make such a child more or less difficult to handle, family organization, and the typical stress periods that the family experience also will be discussed.

The presence of a defective or an impaired child in a family creates a situation that presents a new problem many families have not had to face before. Many have had little experience with the kinds of changes that have to come about in the family structure and orientation in order to deal comfortably with a child who is different in his pattern of development and his behavior and for whom different expectations and goals will be required than those that the parents might have for another child. The reactions of families to the problem of having a deviant child have been classically described by Boyd,[1] Kirk,[2] and Olshansky.[3] In general, one might conceptualize the effect of the less-than-normal child as a disrupting force and a force that has not been dealt with before. *Therefore people have no pattern or model to follow in terms of trying to cope with the situation. It becomes necessary for the family, the parents, and the siblings to develop a strategy to help combat this force and to learn how to deal with the problems that having a retarded child present to their family as individuals and to their family in terms of everyday family life. The goal for the family would be that all family members live comfortably and without undue stress.*

PARENTS' EMOTIONAL REACTIONS AND
THE PROFESSIONAL'S RESPONSE

One of the initial reactions to having a handicapped child is that of denial—denial of the child's handicap or retardation. Denial is a defense mechanism that persons employ to protect themselves from having to suffer the ego deflation of having a defective child. A child represents to a parent an extension of himself; hence it is normal for the parent to perceive any defect of the child as a reflection of his own inadequacies. Actually, many questions could be raised about the denial mechanism. How do persons demonstrate this denial, and how do you as a professional deal with it? Is it an undesirable response?

As was previously stated, denial is a defense mechanism that protects the person from having to see that which would be degrading to his self-concept. This raises a problem concerning the timing for encouraging parents to seek diagnostic evaluations, to see a physician, or to go to the clinic. It is questionable whether parents really profit much from having their child evaluated when they are in the throes of denial. "He can't walk because he hasn't had the opportunity." "There is nothing wrong with Susie; her daddy thinks she is shy." These are some of the responses that parents often have when they are pushed into an evaluation by a grandparent, a public health nurse, or a neighbor before they are really ready to admit and to become aware themselves that the child has some defect or disability. The job at this stage is not to push the parents into a situation in which a professional is telling them that their child is retarded or handicapped but rather to encourage the opportunity for parents to develop beginning self-awareness.

Self-awareness is a very important step that the parent reaches in terms of dealing with the fact that his child is retarded. Recognizing the fact that his child has a problem is perhaps the turning point in the parent's and in the family's ability to deal with the problem. Once this fact is recognized, progress can be made in going on to do something about it. If the recognition or the awareness of the problem never comes, then it typically becomes a matter of abortive attempts on the part of health professionals to do something about a situation that really is not recognized as a problem by the family. When the professional notes that the parents are really not objectively assessing the child's deviation from normal, an effort should be made to help them become aware that their child does have a problem. The nurse can draw attention to how certain behaviors are manifestations of this problem, such as the way the child walks, or his lack of speech, or other aberrant behavior. This action will yield more positive results than will pushing the parents into a situation in which they are being *told* by someone that their child is abnormal. Often the process of planning for and going to visit the professional or a preschool will give the parents a chance to make a comparison of their child with children of similar ages. The point is that the parents need to have the opportunity to deal comfortably with the impact of their child's abnormality. When the diagnosis is thrust on them when they are denying the problem, the result is often one of strengthening the denial process and of promoting hostility toward the professional. Occasionally parents who have been told by a psychologist or a physician that their child's IQ is very low or that he is mentally retarded retort that "The psychologist only spent five minutes with the child," "The child wouldn't perform," or "The child had a cold that day, so how could he know?" The parents often develop hostility toward that professional person, and sometimes other professionals, and usually seek to find more evidence in the child's behavior to prove that the child is not abnormal.

When parents are denying the problem, it stands to reason that attempts to help them work with the child's problem and teach self-help skills stand less chance of success. The parents are neither ready nor are they motivated to plan objectively for their child. Denial is an immobilizing state. Some of the problems parents face at this time can best be summarized in a statement by Solnit and Stark.[4] "Coping with the outer reality of a child with congenital defects and the inner reality of feeling the loss of a desired normal child requires a great deal of mental work. Such psychic work is slow and emotionally painful. It proceeds through the gradual and repeated discharge of intense feelings and memories. These mental and emotional reactions enable the parent to recognize and to adapt to the reality of the retarded child."*

When parents are coming to the recognition of their child's problem, the nurse should offer support by being attentive to clues they are giving about their concerns and questions. They have questions about the child and his behavior, what it means, and what the future holds. How might one intervene and help parents master this phase? This question is worthy of considerable investigation. There are some diagnostic centers that have purposefully planned a prolonged period of evaluation so that the parents will have had the opportunity to come to their own conclusions without having to be told that their child is retarded. *The answer to assisting parents in recognizing and accepting the diagnosis of mental retardation, cerebral palsy, or any handicapping condition lies not so much in careful preparation for telling them that the child is handicapped but more in planning situations that will help them develop their own awareness of the problem, which can then be further interpreted, confirmed, and validated by the professional.*

This beginning awareness leads to a discussion of the frustration that accompanies the passage from denial to self-awareness. As the parents begin to realize that something is wrong with their child, they begin to mull it over in their minds. This often initially occurs through sleepless nights. In the beginning, parents hesitate to communicate their fears to each other; they seem to need to protect one another from the thought and the fear that their child is

---

*From Solnit, A. J., and Stark, M. H.: Mourning and the birth of a defective child, Psychoanal. Stud. Child **16:**523-537, 1961.

handicapped. This is the beginning stage of accepting the fact that their child is not perfect and that there is something wrong with him. As they think about this, there descends a flood of questions to be answered: What is wrong? What caused it? What part did I play? Will I be adequate to handle the situation? Why did God let this happen to me, to my family? What did I do wrong?

At first parents are hesitant to verbalize their questions. Hence the helping person must anticipate their mental turmoil and help initiate the asking. For instance, when one observes the mother and father carefully and almost painfully looking at the 9-month-old child who is not sitting up, but lying placidly on the floor, one might ask: "You are concerned about Jimmy?" This will often open the floodgate of questions and anxieties. Therefore one must be prepared to handle the resulting situation when such a question is asked. It is best not to let the parents expose too much of their concern too quickly. When they do, the result is that they often withdraw from contact with you the next time, feeling that they have revealed too much of their feelings or exposed too much of themselves to someone whom they really didn't know and hadn't learned to trust.

The nurse can control the amount of information the parents expose by limiting the time planned for the visit. It is advisable to make the first contacts with the family brief and let them know in advance that you will be able to see them for only half an hour or an hour. If they seem to be getting into an area that is uncomfortable for them, it might be best to suggest that the particular topic is something they could discuss further on your next visit. The clues indicating that an area is emotionally charged might be a change in the parent's voice quality or pitch, physical restlessness, or a change in facial expression.

Following their awareness of the child's handicap and expression of feelings, the parents come to a point where they can look at their situation more or less objectively. They are ready to seek professional advice. A standard recipe to use in working with all parents does not exist; however, three key points should be considered.

1. All parents need to experience a sense of adequacy in parenting; this is more difficult when one's child is retarded.

2. Parents need to be taught how to work with their handicapped child.

3. Having a retarded child presents a lifelong problem for the child, the parents, and the entire family.

INFLUENCES

Certain influences affect the degree of reaction that the family has as the members go through the process of trying to integrate having a handicapped child into their lives. One of the influences is the sex of the child. Often if the child is a boy and the firstborn, the effect on the family situation is greater because of the high achievement expectations that most parents have for a male child.

It is when parents have relatively high expectations for a child that the necessity of altering these goals for a handicapped child can present additional stress on the parents and family. In this same regard the socioeconomic status of the parents has an influence on how they react to having a retarded child.

Although all families experience more or less the same concerns about day-to-day care and future planning, it is well to keep in mind that the family with high expectations for their children need to talk about and be helped to reformulate their goals for the handicapped child.

Often the parents have to do a great deal of emotional work in terms of dealing with and thinking about the problem. Many times the concern for the future role of the child and how the family will take care of him takes precedence over their dealing with the issue of having a retarded child and what he needs in his or her immediate home environment and home management.

In many families the religious factor is extremely important. It has been found by some investigators[5] that parents who are of the Catholic faith seem to be able to make a quicker adjustment to the fact of having a handicapped child, feeling that this is a responsibility given to them by God. This responsibility is viewed as having merit for the family and one that will actually result in enriching their lives. It is their "cross to bear." They also take comfort that God will give them the strength to deal with this situation. The professional needs to be aware of and utilize the kinds of resources, influences, and inner strengths that parents have in dealing with this difficult problem.

The adjustment of the parents as a couple prior to the birth of the child has a profound effect on how they will handle the situation. If the parents have had a good adjustment, they generally have a better prognosis in terms of their ability to handle a situation in which the child is abnormal. It is believed that it is the husband who has to adapt his family role in such a way as to minimize the conflicting and contradictory demands on his wife. Often in families with retarded children, as well as in families who do not have handicapped children, a phenomenon occurs that can be described as role tension. This means that roles cannot be effectively coordinated. There is no sharp difference between one person's role and another person's role. This can lead to a state of conflict and frustration in their interactions with one another.

Often the husband has to change the expectations that he has of his wife to be a wife, a mother, and a housekeeper. It may necessitate a change in his behavior in terms of helping out more with the children, providing additional emotional support to his wife, and making fewer demands on her. The wife typically has the same demands on her from her husband and other children in the family, in addition to the new demands of care and training of the mentally retarded child. If she is going to be able to meet this composite of demands, there has to be some compromise on the part of the family members in their demands on her.

The degree of the child's deviation is also an important factor. It is difficult for the parents of a child who looks normal and has many normal behaviors to accept the fact that the child is handicapped. It is frustrating to see the deficiencies in the "almost normal" child. In children who have both physical defects and mental retardation, it is sometimes easier for families to make the adjustment, not because it is an easier problem, but because it is visible and can be seen by the parent as well as by others and cannot be denied as easily.

Another influence on parents in dealing with a mentally retarded child is the models they have. Most parents in their parenting role rely on what is offered in books and the mass media, what their parents did with them, or the kinds of things that neighbors do in rearing their children. For parents of normal children there are many, many models, both in the immediate situation, the extended family, and on television. Parents of a handicapped child often have no role models to follow in terms of knowing how to deal with simple self-help skill training for tasks other children "automatically" learn. Parents have questions such as the following: "Do you spread newspapers out on the floor and let the child sit down with a bowl of cereal and a spoon, not caring about the mess?" "Do you continue feeding him because he doesn't seem to want to pick up the spoon and feed himself?" "Do you spank him when he misbehaves?" "Do you take him to the grocery store with you?" "What do you do when people look at you funny?" "What do you do when your child masturbates?"

The nurse can discuss these issues with the parents and many times provide a model of action. As an example, she can demonstrate to the parents how to teach the child a self-help skill such as feeding or how to set certain limits.

REFERENCES

1. Boyd, D.: The three stages in the growth of a parent of a mentally retarded child, Amer. J. Ment. Defic. **55**:608-611, 1951.
2. Kirk, S.: You and your retarded child, New York, 1955, The Macmillan Co.
3. Olshansky, S.: Chronic sorrow: a response to having a mentally defective child, Soc. Casework **43**:191-194, 1962.
4. Solnit, A. J., and Stark, M. H.: Mourning and the birth of a defective child, Psychoanal. Stud. Child **16**:523-537, 1961.
5. Zuk, G. H., Miller, R. L., Bortram, J. B., and Kling, F.: Maternal acceptance of retarded children: a questionnaire study of attitudes and religious background, Child Develop. **32**:525-540, 1961.

ADDITIONAL READINGS

Auerback, A. B.: Group education for parents of the handicapped, Children **8:**135-140, 1961.

Barnard, K. E.: Teaching the retarded child is a family affair, Amer. J. Nurs. **68:**305-311, 1968.

Baun, M.: Some dynamic factors affecting family adjustment to the handicapped child, Exceptional Child. **28:**387-391, 1962.

Cohen, P.: The impact of the handicapped child on the family, Soc. Casework **43:**137-142, 1962.

Dalton, J., and Epstein, H.: Counseling parents of mildly retarded children, Soc. Casework **44:**523-530, 1963.

De Young, C. D.: Nursing contribution in family crisis, Nurs. Outlook **16:**60-62, 1968.

Dittmann, L. L.: The mentally retarded child at home: a manual for parents, Washington, D. C., 1959, U. S. Department of Health, Education, and Welfare, Children's Bureau Publication No. 374.

Forbes, N.: The nurse and genetic counseling, Nursing Clinics of North America, Philadelphia, December, 1966, W. B. Saunders Co.

Graliker, B. V., Fishler, K., and Koch, R.: Teenage reaction to a mentally retarded sibling, Amer. J. Ment. Defic. **66:**838-843, 1962.

Haar, D. J.: Improved phenylketonuric diet control through group education of mothers, Nursing Clinics of North America, Philadelphia, 1966, W. B. Saunders Co.

Jensen, R. A.: The clinical management of the mentally retarded child and the parents, Amer. J. Psychiat. **106:**830-833, 1950.

Keogh, B., and Legeay, C.: Recoil from the diagnosis of mental retardation, Amer. J. Nurs. **66:**778-780, 1966.

Logan, H.: My child is mentally retarded, Nurs. Outlook **10:**445-448, 1962.

Marschak, M.: A method for evaluating child-parent interaction, J. Genet. Psychol. **97:**3-22, 1960.

Michaels, J., and Schueman, H.: Observations on the psychodynamics of parents of retarded children, Amer. J. Ment. Defic. **66:**568-573, 1962.

Miller, L. G.: Toward a greater understanding of the parents of the mentally retarded child, J. Pediat. **73:**699-705, 1968.

Milligan, G. E.: Counseling parents of the mentally retarded: a review of literature, Ment. Retard. Abstr. **2:**259-264, July-Sept., 1965.

Murray, M. A.: Needs of the parents of M. R. children, Amer. J. Ment. Defic. **63:**1078-1088, 1959.

Parad, H. J., and Caplan, G.: A framework for studying families in crisis. In Parad, H. J., editor: Crisis intervention: selected readings, New York, 1965, Family Service Association of America.

Pattullo, A.: Puberty in the girl who is retarded, New York, 1969, National Association for Retarded Children.

Raech, H.: A parent discusses initial counseling, Ment. Retard. **4:**25-26, 1966.

4
Family organization and strategy development

FAMILY LIFE CYCLE

In thinking about how the family deals with having a handicapped child, it is important to look at the family as a functioning unit. Having a mentally retarded child presents a family crisis.

Farber,[1] a sociologist, describes the family as a set of mutually contingent careers. A career is defined as a progression of roles that unfolds in a patterned sequence in a life cycle, beginning with marriage and ending with the deaths of the spouses. Movement in the cycle is stimulated by a change in the career of the children, which causes a shift in the roles of parents and a redefinition of values in accordance with conventional norms. The stages in family development that produce role changes in the family unit are as follows:

1. Families with no children
2. Families with infant children
3. Families with preschool children
4. Families with elementary school children
5. Families with junior high school and high school children
6. Families with college-age children
7. Families whose children have since left home or married [2]

The movement in these stages and the roles that parents and children play are definitely influenced by the changes that occur in the growth and development of the children. This becomes painfully clear to parents in the case of the handicapped child. When the child is mentally retarded, he does not pass through the normal changing careers or roles. There is a great deal of sameness day by day. The family has to be helped to move along in the normal cycle of a family's development in spite of the lack of change in the day-by-day dependency that is seen in the child. It is important that one attend to how the family is organized, their goals and values, when evaluating what they are doing and the problems they are having.

STRATEGY DEVELOPMENT

In studying family organization, Farber[1] evaluated 233 families. The families had the following characteristics: (1) the parents were Caucasian, (2) the mentally retarded child was under 16 years of age, (3) the parents were married and living together, and (4) the child was the product of the present marriage and the only severely retarded child in the family.

Eighty-three of the families were identified as having a definite strategy. In other words, the parents were in agreement about the basic goals for which they were working and arranged their roles within the family to facilitate the achievement of these goals. As one might suspect, the families with a definable strategy demonstrated a significantly higher level of marital integration. Marital integration was measured by the degree of role tension between husband and wife and their agreement or disagreement on domestic values.

What does this mean? It suggests the necessity of looking at how families are progressing in their normal career pattern. When a halting effect is noted, efforts should be made to help the parents more clearly identify their goals and arrange their own roles and relationships to assist the family in achieving their goals.

The three types of strategies described by Farber are presented, since they provide a conceptual framework that can guide your assessment and support of the family. The strategies are titled in relation to the persons whose demands and needs are given priority in family life. The major orientation and general characteristics of each strategy are summarized.

Child-oriented strategy

Basic goal: Parents agree that the most important task in family life is the maintenance of the family unit.

General characteristics
1. Children are highly valued. The boys' achievements are particularly stressed.
2. Activities are directed toward fulfilling the needs of the children.
3. The children are the main bond between the husband and the wife.
4. There is a sharp division of labor. The husband is oriented toward economic pursuits, whereas the wife's focus is on domestic matters.
5. Both parents receive most of their emotional support from outside the nuclear family.
6. Participation in the community, although extremely important, is directed toward fulfilling the demands and needs of the children.

Home-oriented strategy

Basic goal: Maintenance of family continuity; however, this is accomplished by withdrawing from striving in middle-class endeavors.

General characteristics
1. The internal structure of the family is emphasized rather than its relation to extrafamily groups.
2. The husband is the central figure in the family in his role of economic provider and social-emotional leader in the family.
3. Although the wife looks to the husband for emotional support, the husband seeks support from all family members.

4. Children are highly valued.
5. Happiness, creativity, and mental health of the children are emphasized rather than achievement.
6. Community participation is elected on the basis of personal interest rather than social mobility.

Parent-oriented strategy

Basic goal: Orientation toward achievement of the husband in the middle-class society.

General characteristics

1. Family life is built around achievement, personal development, and social skills for the parents and also the children, regardless of sex.
2. The parents operate as partners in relation to the economic and domestic tasks; the wife is active in community participation important to the husband's success. The husband, in compensation, is active in social-emotional tasks of the family.
3. The wife expresses some resentment at the demanding nature of motherhood.
4. The parents rely on community and extrafamily support.
5. The parents are concerned with their life careers and tend to view the retarded child as an interruption in terms of the child's effect on their plans.

It is important to look at how the family is already beginning to deal with their problems before an outsider imposes his way of handling them. A case that illustrates this concept is that of a young couple with a severely retarded child. The young child needed surgery to lengthen tight heel cords. At the same time the father was trying to advance his own professional attainment in terms of becoming an airline pilot. Therefore there were two demands for money simultaneously, one for the father's flying lessons and the second for the child's surgery. It was necessary for the parents to pay for the surgery because in this situation, as with many children who have congenital defects, the child was not covered by insurance. The nurse realized, in looking carefully at how this family dealt with problems and also what their goals were, that the father's progress and achievement were very important. She supported the parents' decision on the immediate use of money to advance his career. In the course of time the child's surgery did take place and importantly the parents felt good about what they had done and the accomplishments that had been made toward the goals that they had for their family and themselves as parents. A conflict possibly would have resulted if the nurse had continued to push for the child's surgery because of her concern that this be done. It was most important for the nurse to look at the total family situation and see just how the parents were working to attain their own values and goals and then to work within this pattern.

There is little argument that the presence of a retarded individual in a family presents personal-social conflict for the family members. Society values beauty, intelligence, and productiveness. These specific values are violated to some degree by every retarded individual. Parents have described the process by which they experience or anticipate the halting effect of a retarded child's decelerated development on their own life career. For instance, it has been reported that families have a subsequent drop in birthrate when a defective child has been identified. Mothers have been known to alter their whole pattern of behavior and devote exclusive attention to the defective child. Because of the unpredictable development of the child, it becomes difficult for these families to anticipate the course of their family's development. This unpredictability refers especially to the period of time when children are grown and move from the family's shelter, both emotionally and economically. Parents of retarded children encounter a set of circumstances different from those of other parents. It is for this reason that they must develop a plan that enables their family to handle the problem and effectively develop both personal and family goals.

In helping the parents develop a plan, it is important to consider their goals. Do they seek primarily to attain success and achievement for themselves or for the children? In accomplishing their goal, is there stress on their companionship as parents or the continuity of the family? Is there an agreement between the parents concerning who provides economically for the family and who focuses on domestic matters? Where does the family seek emotional support? How much do family members participate in the community and for what reasons?

The following list of questions[3] provides suggestions as to some of the areas on which it is important to focus to help understand better how the family is organized and how the retarded child affects the family.

1. When did you find out for certain what the problem really was?

2. Have you been told if your child will be able to go to school or what do you expect his or her future to be?

3. How did the children react when they found out that something was different about their brother or sister?

4. Have you noticed any change in the disposition of your other children?

5. Has your child affected the children's relationships outside the home and if so, how?

6. Has there been any change in your daily way of living, such as eating, shopping, sleeping, or the general home atmosphere?

7. Have there been changes in things you do as a family, such as picnics, vacations, and family projects?

8. Have any of the plans or goals of the family had to be changed?

9. Would you say that your child requires a lot of care?

10. Have you ever thought about placing your child in an institution?

11. How well would you say you as parents agree on the best way to handle your child?

12. How much alike are you as husband and wife in the things you think are important in life for the family, like religious training, plans, goals for the children, or getting ahead?

13. Have you noticed any change in your dispositions?

14. Have you found you are able to talk with each other about your concerns and worries?

15. How has your health been?

16. Do you feel that you have had to restrict your activities outside the home? Neighborhood?

17. Are you neighborly?

18. Do you find that any of your relatives are unkind to or critical of your child?

19. Do you feel that there are any things that you as a husband or wife are doing to keep from facing some of the problems in dealing with the child?

20. How do you feel about the progress you have made in the past year in learning how to handle or take care of the child?

21. What do you foresee as problems that you still need to work on?

STRESS PERIODS

There are certain periods that provide more stressful situations for the parents and the family of the mentally retarded child than other times, and it is during these periods that intervention or supportive assistance can probably be the most meaningful. One of the first stress periods occurs when the parent is developing awareness that his child is handicapped or deviant. Often a parent does this alone. It has been reported by parents that when they have had questions about their child's development and sought the advice of a professional person such as a physician, this concern has been met with a response such as, "Oh, he'll grow out of it. He'll be all right." The parent, sensing something is wrong, is told not to worry. This represents false assurance and presents even more conflict for the parent. Often parents describe how they were encouraged by relatives to take some action, the relatives pointing out the child's disability.

There is a definite necessity to learn more about what happens to parents when they are coming to an awareness that their child has a problem. Some professionals believe that it interferes with the mother-child relationship if the mother finds out about the child's problem very soon after his birth, as in the case of the child born with mongolism, in which the physical characteristics are readily apparent. Nurses should give support during this period when the parents are "finding out" and help them find resources in terms of both people and services that will show them that there are facilities and programs that can handle the kinds of problems their child represents. They also may profit from knowing and being able to talk with parents who have children with similar handicaps. This establishes in their minds that they are not alone, that there are other persons with normal intelligence, with normal family backgrounds, and with normal desires and needs who have the same type of problem—thus they are not some kind of freak. It is very reassuring to them to be able to talk with these other parents to find out how they handled the problem. These parents provide the models that are so important to them in terms of child rearing. Group experiences provide many benefits for parents. Nursing must continue to move into the area of working with groups of parents.

Another period of stress arises when the ordinary child-rearing practices do not work, for example, when parents try to handle a child, as in the feeding experience, in a way similar to one that worked with their other children. When their attempts to feed the child are frustrated by his responses of not taking in food, not being able to suck, not sitting still in the highchair, etc., they need to have help in knowing what to do, how to change the environment, or how to manage their parenting behavior to get a better response from the child.

Getting information from professional people can often be a crisis or stress period for parents. One common problem is that parents may experience stress or crisis while waiting for or going through the process of getting information from professionals. Parents are often not sure what questions are appropriate to ask, what kinds of information they need to know, and what kinds of resources are available. The nurse can do a great deal to prepare the parents for their visit with a physician. In the case of a child who has hydrocephalus, for example, the nurse can help by writing out some specific questions that the parents should ask such as, "Will the head get any bigger?" The nurse can help with the proper terminology the parents need to use so that they can converse with the physician. She can help them to remember to call to the physician's attention the constipation that the child has and remind them to ask about the child's developmental or IQ level. The nurse can prepare herself by knowing the type of information provided by the physician, the psychologist, the speech and hearing person, so that parents might profit in the best possible way from their contacts with these people.

The nurse can seek out community resources for dealing with stressful problems at various stages of the child's development. Presently in most parts of the United States there are resources for young retarded children, and many schools have special education classes for the children of elementary school age. One of the deficiencies in services is adequate resources for persons 15 years of age and older. Sheltered workshops and day-care centers that would provide recreation for severely and moderately retarded or handicapped children are especially needed. The nurse might share the responsibility of helping the parents find these resources. If they are not available in the community, she can actually help the parents press a voluntary agency into undertaking such a project. She might lobby members of her state legislature on the need to develop certain types of resources.

When a new sibling is born into a family with a mentally retarded child, the new baby presents a stress. Often during this time the parents' feelings about the handicapped child undergo reexamination. For instance, they may have been able to give the child enough attention before, but now with a new baby in the family, they may be concerned about how they are going to divide their attention between their new normal baby and their retarded or handicapped child.

Another situation that causes frustration for the parents is explaining to the other children the fact that one child is retarded, is handicapped, or is different. Explaining and helping the other children understand that their brother or sister is not normal is a recurring source of concern for the parents. Parents ask how to explain why their demands on the handicapped child may be different from their demands on the other children.

In summary, the stress periods for families of retarded children are as follows:

1. When they are finding out what the child's problem is and what this means for them as parents and a family
2. When ordinary child-rearing practices don't work
3. When getting information from professional people
4. When they need to find appropriate community resources
5. When siblings are confronted with differences in their brother or sister or a new sibling is born
6. School placement
7. Adolescence

SUPPORT TO FAMILIES

What are the significant ways in which families who have handicapped children can be helped? Parents of normal children often ponder whether in this complex society they will be adequate in child rearing, even though they have many role models to imitate and from whom to derive support. The parents of a retarded child remain more or less isolated in meeting the problems because of the child's slower rate of development, his lack of responsiveness, or his excessive undesirable behavior. Following are some of the ways in which nurses can help families of handicapped children:

1. By helping the parents learn how to assess the child's ability and then plan for promoting optimal development (breaking a task into its component parts).

2. By encouraging communication with both parents. One of the ways of encouraging this communication with both parents is to make it a principle that you communicate with them as a couple rather than with the mother or father alone. Encourage them continually to share and to solve their problems together.

3. By giving them information that they would find interesting and useful. Anticipate the questions they need to be asking of you, of the physician, of the social worker, of the teacher, of the dentist, and of the physical therapist.

4. By talking about the future and encouraging hope. If parents do not have the hope that things will change, that their child will improve, then they will become even more discouraged and dismayed.

5. By providing opportunities to meet parents with similar situations. Groups not only save your professional time but also, perhaps more importantly, do a great deal to meet the needs of the parents.

6. By encouraging the development of resources in your community to assist parents of handicapped children with their task of child rearing. Schools, day-care centers, therapy centers, and halfway houses are all appropriate adjuncts to the family's efforts to care for the retarded child.

7. By providing anticipatory support for the stress periods they will experience on a successive basis.

Once the family's general orientation has been identified, in other words, their values and their goals, steps should be taken to increase the agreement the parents have on their values pertaining to family life. Recommendations should be made as to appropriate action to be taken with respect to matters of relationships with their parents and friends, division of labor between the parents, the place of children in the family, and the solution of specific husband-and-wife problems. It is important for the helping person to work within the family strategy, strengthening it and not imposing recommendations foreign to their orientation or method of problem solving. Some practical considerations are evident in terms of the nurse being able to use these principles in evaluating a family's functioning and also in knowing how best to direct her intervention. If, for instance, the family fits the characteristic of a home-oriented family, one interested in maintaining a happy home environment, she would make a recommendation that would fit in with utilizing the strengths of the family and environment, such as in providing play experience for a preschool child. It would probably be more appropriate and consistent with this family's orientation to suggest that the family work with the child at home and bring in some other children for the child to play with rather than their seeking a community play center or nursery school.

When the family is in the process of redefining the child as a child with a handicap, it is important that they do not define the child in a sick role. The sick role generally implies much less expectation of independence. The professional person working with the family can provide many sources of direction once the basic orientation and stage of family development have been determined. Here, as in working with specific behavioral management, the most important step is to observe the kinds of things that are happening and the values and goals that the family has, then work within that framework.

REFERENCES

1. Farber, B.: Family and crisis: maintenance of integration in families with a severely mentally retarded child, Monographs of the Society for Research in Child Development, 1960, No. 1, Serial 75.
2. Duvall, E. R.: Family development, Chicago, 1957, J. B. Lippincott Co.
3. Zelle, R.: A study to determine the need for a conceptual guide to assess the effect of a retarded child on family relations and life, unpublished master's thesis, University of Washington, 1969.

ADDITIONAL READINGS

Barsch, R. H.: The parent of the handicapped child: the study of child rearing practices, Springfield, Ill., 1968, Charles C Thomas, Publisher.
Farber, B.: Interaction with retarded siblings and life goals of children, Marriage and Family Living 25:96-98, 1963.
Farber, B., and Ryckman, D. B.: Effects of severely mentally retarded children on family relationships, Ment. Retard. Abstr. 2:1-17, Jan.-March, 1965.
Legeay, C., and Keogh, B.: Impact of mental retardation on family life, Amer. J. Nurs. 66:1062-1065, 1966.
Wolf, I. S.: Nursing role in counseling parents of mentally retarded children, Washington, D. C., 1967, U. S. Department of Health, Education, and Welfare.
Wolfensberger, W.: Counseling the parents of the retarded. In Baumeister, A. A., editor: Mental retardation: appraisal, education and rehabilitation, Chicago, 1967, Aldine Publishing Co.
Wolfensberger, W., and Kurtz, R. A., editors. Management of the family of the mentally retarded: a book of readings, Chicago, 1969, Follett Education Corporation.

section three
METHODS OF ASSESSMENT AND OBSERVATION

5

Assessing the child's development and functioning

Important factors in any professional relationship are the development of rapport and clarification of role. This is certainly true of the nurse's relationships with families of retarded children.

The point at which the nurse makes contact with the family varies. The parents may have just had the child evaluated or it may be the nurse's observations that lead to a referral for evaluation. The parents need to know in what way the nurse can assist them in developing their methods of handling and teaching the child so that he can reach further goals in his development. She will want to explain also the need for talking about how they are currently handling the child and for actually observing his behavior.

In arranging for a home visit, it is well to schedule a time when both parents are at home and the child is awake. Prior to the interview the available data (medical history, previous evaluations and services, comments by teachers or other professionals) should be reviewed for clues to the special nature of the problem. Questions may then be asked and observations made at the interview to verify and further investigate the nature of the problem indicated in the initial information.

To help the parents plan or change their approach, the nurse will have to obtain information on the general behavior of the child, his developmental level, the parents' teaching practices, and family interactions. Four general approaches in getting this information are as follows:

1. Parent interview guide
2. Developmental assessment
3. Behavioral observations
4. Play observation

PARENT INTERVIEW GUIDE

It is helpful first to find out how the parent sees the situation. The previous section, "Family Considerations," presented ways to elicit information on the effects the child has on the family. The focus in this chapter is on the child's functioning within the family.

Questions asked of the parents should be arranged so that the responses furnish, insofar as possible, an in-depth picture of the developmental level of the child, the nature of his environment, his interactions within it, and the family's functioning.

Since interviews vary in their immediate purpose and the surrounding circumstances, the range of questions and observations will vary with each interview situation. The questions asked should be dependent on the age of the child, his history, and the nurse's observations. It would not be possible to compile a complete list of questions and observations that would be universally applicable. Consideration of the following topics, however, should be helpful in planning the interview. These questions are of importance in relation to the retarded child.

An appropriate beginning topic is feeding.

Feeding: At what times does the family eat? Is the child allowed to help prepare his food? Whom does he sit next to at mealtime? Is he allowed to leave the table before finishing? When does he use a spoon? Is it difficult to tolerate his messiness when he is learning to eat? What do parents expect of him in the way of table manners? Do they have a clean-plate policy? Is he allowed to interrupt adult conversation at the table? When he does something parents do not allow, how do they handle it?

Sleep: Where does he sleep? How far from the parents' room? What time does he go to bed at night? What time does he awaken? How many hours does he usually sleep at night? Any trouble getting him up? Does he awaken during the night? How often? What are the possible causes? What do they do about it? How often does he take naps? How long are they? Does he resist going to bed? How is this handled?

Play: What are his favorite toys? Pull toys? Wind-up toys? Noisemakers? Building toys? How long does he play with a specific toy? Who are his favorite play companions? Does he prefer older or younger children? In what types of games or activities do they engage? Is he included in others' play? What happens if another child takes his toy? Is he allowed to take another child's toy at play? How does he imitate parents in their household duties? What are some typical examples of how he imitates his father? How does he get along with siblings? How much TV is he allowed to watch? What are his favorite programs? Does he watch to the end of the program? What is his behavior like on a swing? What does he do if he loses his balance? Can he jump? Can he guide and pedal a tricycle? At what time of day do parents play with him just for their own pleasure? Ask the parents to share something about this.

Toileting: Request that parents describe his bathroom routines. Does he use the regular toilet or his own potty? Are there ever any accidents? What methods have been used to train him? What has been effective? What has not been successful? Are parents going to attempt a program again? What methods have they thought of? Do they think these will work?

Dressing: What articles of clothing does he remove by himself? When does he help dress himself? Are there any articles he has particular trouble getting in or out of? Does he button and unbutton? Does he unsnap-snap? Unzip-zip? Unlace-lace? Unbuckle-buckle? Untie-tie? Does he get the front of the garment in front? Shoes on right feet? Does he have any preferences for what he wears?

Toothbrushing: Does he have a toothbrush? How does he handle it? When are his teeth brushed?

Household responsibilities: What are his regular tasks? Which of these does he enjoy? What are the tasks he does not like? Is he included in such activities as yard work?

Discipline: Reassure parents that getting children to mind is often a problem. How do the parents go about getting their children to mind? What are the differences with the child with whom we are concerned? When was the last time they found it necessary to discipline their child? Is he responsive to the word "no"? Is he ever scolded for anything? What kinds of things? How effective is scolding? Most parents spank their children at one time or another. Have the parents give examples of times when they spank. Does it work? Do they ever take away something they know he really enjoys when he does something they do not like? Do they ever make him stay in his room or on a chair? How do they reward him for good behavior? Remind mother that some parents, for example, use gold stars, points, or money. Have the parents describe the kinds of things he has been praised for in the past week. In what areas of child rearing do the parents disagree? Ask the parents to describe the child's reaction when he does not get what he wants. Ask the parents to share their thoughts about what concerns them most regarding the child's behavior at home.

This parent interview guide is designed to gain significant information about how a concern is viewed, what has been done about it, and what parents intend to do in the future. Responses from parents will reveal the following:

1. A pattern that indicates use of or lack of a consistent approach in dealing with a problem
2. Use of or lack of imitative models
3. Parental expectations of a child's performance
4. A description of the teaching environment
5. Characteristic patterns of the child's reactions to others
6. Methods that have been tried, those that have worked, those that have failed, and parents' willingness or readiness to approach a problem again
7. The responses of others to the child's behavior

DEVELOPMENTAL ASSESSMENT

It is necessary to observe children directly to assess functional levels. This is done also to find out what is easy for children and what is not so easy for them. Verbal reports are not sufficient but may be used in conjunction with watching a child being fed, eating, undressing, dressing, playing, responding to commands, practicing fine and gross motor skills, toileting, or preparing for bedtime.

The *Washington Guide for Promoting Development in the Young Child* is presented in this book to give one framework that can be used in making developmental assessments. This guide was specifically designed to assist nurses in doing a better job in observing, assessing, case finding, and planning developmental interventions for infants and children. The guide helps a nurse to be more objective about the information she is obtaining.

Using such a guide requires direct observations of a child's specific behaviors. The method of relying heavily on direct observations helps reduce some of the inherent weaknesses of relying on others' reports of developmental tasks that they believe a child can or cannot accomplish. The organization of the *Washington Guide* is characterized by a distinct sequential format. Developmental items are arranged in an orderly way, giving a progressive guide of simple to complex tasks that are expected of a child in his development at different age periods. It is also characterized by the way in which it structures a one-to-one relationship, that is, information is derived from the nurse interacting on a one-to-one basis with a child to elicit certain behaviors. It requires getting down to the child's level for closer observations and interactions.

This guide is used to observe well infants and children, those suspected of developmental delays, and those with known high-risk factors in their development. The guide is used in a variety of settings such as well-child clinics, child development centers, maternal and infant projects, day-care centers, institutions, pediatric floors in hospitals, physicians' offices, schools, and private homes.

The data gained from the guide are used as a basis for reassuring mothers of their children's development, counseling mothers on expectations, offering anticipatory guidance, and giving suggestions in promoting development, and can serve as a guideline for referral and a longitudinal record for ongoing developmental assessments.

As with any tool, both strengths and weaknesses are apparent. The *Washington Guide* has not been standardized on a population sample. The developmental items that comprise the expected tasks at various ages from newborn to 5 years of age are considered valid. The sources utilized as references in constructing the composite of items found in the *Washington Guide* are listed at the end of the chapter.

There are a number of screening tools available, such as the *Denver Developmental Screening Test,* which primarily provide a means of identifying the significant variances in child development. The *Washington Guide* differs from these in that it is not specifically designed to be used as a screening tool; its primary purpose is to present a frame of reference about growth and development that will enable the nurse to observe a child's abilities systematically and on that basis make recommendations regarding child-rearing practices that would capitalize on the child's present abilities and encourage further movement up the developmental ladder. In summary, the purpose of the *Washington Guide* is to provide a reference for the nurse to use in observing development, giving parental counseling, or making appropriate referrals for evaluation. Refer to the Appendix for further discussion of developmental screening tools.

Through observations the nurse initially determines where the child is functioning developmentally. The significant services given by nurses to parents who have children with developmental deviations consist essentially of assisting the family to learn to appraise a child's developmental status and thus guide parental expectations, discipline, and training to the functional level to promote optimal development of the child.

SUGGESTIONS FOR USING THE *WASHINGTON GUIDE*

A few suggestions regarding the structure and use of the guide will provide the nurse with enough information to use it.

1. The guide follows the structure of the most common functional activities of the young child's daily life—feeding, sleep, play, language, motor activities, discipline, toilet training, and dressing. In each category of activity, the developmental attainments that would be expected in accord with references on child development are grouped as "Expected Tasks" within a three-month age range during the first twelve months of life, then at six- to twelve-month intervals until 5 years of age. Accompanying each category and age grouping of "expected tasks" is a listing of "suggested activities" that can serve as the basis of advice to the parents about enriching child-rearing practices.

2. There are no criteria established for the administration and scoring of items. The references that follow this chapter provide information of this nature.

3. There are no requirements for specific equipment or elaborate monitoring systems. The toys and equipment in the child's natural environment should be relied on.

4. In using the guide, it is suggested that you

    a. Familiarize yourself with the appropriate age grouping of the child to be observed.

    b. Start below the child's chronological age level, so that success with tasks can be experienced from the beginning.

c. Whenever possible, observe the child's performance.

d. Ask the parents to relay information about the item when this is not possible.

e. Carefully explain to the parents that you will be going from easy to difficult tasks.

f. Ask the parent to refrain from prompting or interfering with the child's attempt to carry out a request.

g. Cross out or note on a separate recording each item the child can do; this leaves you with listings of the target areas that represent possible points for making use of the "suggested activities."

h. List appropriate suggested activities and discuss them with the parents.

5. A precise numerical rating or score of the child's behavior is not sought. However, through directly observing the child in a series of activities, a functional age range can be established.

It is recommended that a child be considered as functioning at a particular age range if he is doing a majority of the tasks in that grouping. The guide is arranged so that you have ready access to both the preceding and following age groupings. If a child is doing none of the tasks within an age range, refer to the previous ages; in instances in which the child has completed all activities in an age grouping, proceed to a more advanced grouping.

6. After the age-range skills a child can perform are eliminated, the target areas or deficits in development that should be strengthened are automatically visible. The suggestions for activities that correspond to the identified target areas can then be used as a beginning point of teaching the parent how he can specifically enhance the attainment of developmental skills.

The guide is presented in its entirety. It should be noted that: *this tool is not expected to give you precise information on the child's developmental level. The* Washington Guide to Promoting Development in the Young Child *will assist you in observing the child on a systematic basis, point out variations in development, and give you suggestions regarding appropriate child-rearing practices.*

THE WASHINGTON GUIDE TO PROMOTING DEVELOPMENT IN THE YOUNG CHILD

MOTOR SKILLS

Expected tasks	Suggested activities
1 to 3 months	
1. Holds head up briefly when prone	1. Place infant in prone position
2. Head erect and bobbing when supported in sitting position	2. Support in sitting position with his head erect

3. Head erect and steady in sitting position
4. Follows object through all planes
5. Palmar grasp
6. Moro reflex

3. Pull infant to sitting position
4. Provide with opportunity to observe people or activity
5. Hang bright-colored objects and mobiles within reach across crib
6. Provide with opportunity to observe objects or people while in sitting position
7. Use infant seat
8. Alternate bright shiny objects with dark and light visual patterns

4 to 8 months

1. Sits with minimal support, with stable head and back
2. Sits alone steadily
3. Plays with hands, which are open most of time
4. Grasps rattle or bottle with both hands
5. Picks up small objects, i.e., cube
6. Transfers toys from one hand to other
7. Neck-righting reflex

1. Pull up to sitting position
2. Provide opportunity to sit supported or alone when head and trunk control are stabilized
3. Put bright-colored objects within reach
4. Give toys or household objects: rattles, teething ring, cloth animals or dolls, 1-inch cubes, plastic objects such as cups, rings, and balls
5. Offer small objects such as cereal to improve grasp
6. Offer a variety of patterns or textures to play with
7. Use squeak toys

9 to 12 months

1. Rises to sitting position
2. Creeps or crawls, maybe backward at first
3. Pulls to standing position
4. Stands alone
5. Cruises
6. Uses index finger to poke
7. Finger-thumb grasp
8. Parachute reflex
9. Landau reflex

1. Provide playpen, allow child to pull himself to standing
2. Give opportunity and space to practice creeping and crawling
3. Have child practice moving on knees to improve balance prior to walking
4. Have child use walker or straddle toys
5. Play airplane with child; have child practice catching himself while rolling on large ball
6. Provide with objects such as spoons, plastic bottles, cups, ball, cubes, finger foods, saucepans, and lids

13 to 18 months

1. Walks a few steps without support
2. Balanced when walking
3. Walks upstairs with help, creeps downstairs
4. Turns pages of book

1. Provide opportunity to practice walking, climbing stairs with help
2. Give toys that can be pushed around
3. Supervise activity with paper and large crayons

MOTOR SKILLS—cont'd

Expected tasks	Suggested activities

13-18 months—cont'd

4. Provide toys such as cubes, cups, sauce-pans, lids, rag dolls, and other soft, cuddly toys
5. Begin introducing child to swing

19 to 30 months

1. Runs
2. Walks up and down stairs, one at a time (not alternating feet)
3. Imitates vertical strokes
4. Imitates building tower of four or more blocks
5. Throws ball overhand
6. Jumps in place
7. Rides tricycle

1. Needs opportunity to practice and develop activities
2. Provide pattern for child while he watches and then encourage him to try
3. Provide tricycle or similar pedal toys; secure foot on pedal if necessary

31 to 48 months

1. Walks downstairs (alternating feet)
2. Hops on one foot
3. Swings and climbs
4. Balances on one foot for 10 seconds
5. Copies circle
6. Copies cross
7. Draws person with three parts

1. Continue with blocks, combining materials, toy cars, and trains
2. Provide clay and other manipulating materials
3. Give opportunities to swing and climb
4. Provide with activities such as finger painting, chalk, and blackboard

49 to 52 months

1. Balances well
2. Skips and jumps
3. Can heel-toe walk
4. Copies square
5. Catches bounced ball

1. Provide with music and games to synchronize hand and foot, tapping with music, skipping, hopping, and dancing rhythmically to improve coordination

FEEDING SKILLS

Expected tasks	Suggested activities

1 to 3 months

1. Sucking reflex present
2. Rooting reflex present
3. Ability to swallow pureed foods
4. Coordinates sucking, swallowing, and breathing

1. Consider a change in nipple or posturing if there is difficulty in swallowing
2. Introduce solids, one kind at a time (use small spoon, place food well back on infant's tongue)
3. Hold in comfortable relaxed position while feeding
4. Pace feeding tempo to infant's needs

4 to 8 months

1. Tongue used in moving food in mouth
2. Hand-to-mouth motions

1. Give finger foods to develop chewing, stimulate gums, and encourage hand

Expected tasks	Suggested activities

3. Recognizes bottle on sight
4. Gums or mouths solid foods
5. Feeds self cracker

-to-mouth motion (cubes of cheese, bananas, dry toast, bread crust, cookies)
2. Encourage upright supported position for feeding
3. Promote bottle holding
4. Introduce junior foods

9 to 12 months

1. Holds own bottle
2. Drinks from cup or glass with assistance
3. Finger feeds
4. Beginning to hold spoon

1. Bring child in highchair to table and include in part of or entire meal with family
2. Have child in dry comfortable position with trunk and feet supported
3. Encourage self-help in feeding; use of table foods
4. Offer spoon when interest is indicated
5. Introduce cup or glass with small amount of fluid

13 to 18 months

1. Holds cup and handle with digital grasp
2. Lifts cup and drinks well
3. Beginning to use spoon, may turn bowl down before reaching mouth
4. Difficulty in inserting spoon into mouth
5. May refuse food

1. Continue offering finger foods (wieners, sandwiches)
2. Use nontip dishes and cups; dishes should have sides to make filling of spoon easy
3. Give opportunity for self-feeding
4. Provide fluids between meals rather than having child fill up on fluids at mealtime

19 to 30 months

1. Drinks without spilling
2. Holds small glass in one hand
3. Inserts spoon in mouth correctly
4. Distinguishes between food and inedible material
5. Plays with food

1. Encourage self-feeding with spoon
2. Do not rush child
3. Serve foods plainly but in attractive servings
4. Small servings of food will encourage eating more than large servings

31 to 48 months

1. Pours well from pitcher
2. Serves self at table with little spilling
3. Rarely needs assistance
4. Interest in setting table

1. Encourage self-help
2. Give opportunity for pouring (give rice and pitcher to promote pouring skills)
3. Encourage child to help set table
4. Have well-defined rules about table manners

49 to 52 months

1. Feeds self well
2. Social and talkative during meal

1. Socialize with child at mealtime
2. Have child help with preparation, table setting, and serving

FEEDING SKILLS—cont'd

<table>
<tr><td>Expected tasks</td><td>Suggested activities</td></tr>
</table>

49-52 months—cont'd

3. Include child in conversations at mealtimes by planning special times for him to tell about events, situations, or what he did during day

SLEEP

Expected tasks	Suggested activities

1 to 3 months

1. Night: 4 to 10-hour intervals
2. Naps: frequent
3. Longer periods of wakefulness without crying

1. Provide separate sleeping arrangements away from parents' room
2. Reduce noise and light stimulation when placing in bed
3. Have room at comfortable temperature with no drafts or extremes in heat
4. Reverse position of crib occasionally
5. Place child in different positions from time to time for sleep
6. Alternate from back to side to stomach
7. Keep crib sides up

4 to 8 months

1. Night: 10 to 12 hours
2. Naps: 2 to 3 (1 to 4 hours in duration)
3. Night awakenings

1. Keep crib sides up
2. Refrain from taking child into parents' room if he awakens
3. Check to determine if there is cause for awakenings: hunger, teething, pain, cold, wet, noise, or illness
4. If a baby-sitter is used, attempt to find some person with whom infant is familiar. Explain bedtime and naptime arrangements

9 to 12 months

1. Night: 12 to 14 hours
2. Naps: 1 to 2 (1 to 4 hours in duration)
3. May begin refusing morning nap

1. Short crying periods may be source of tension release for child
2. Observe for signs of fatigue, irritability, or restlessness if naps are shorter
3. Provide familiar person to baby-sit who knows sleep routines

13 to 18 months

1. Night: 10 to 12 hours
2. Naps: one in afternoon (1 to 3 hours in duration)

1. Night terrors may be terminated by awakening infant and offering reassurance

Expected tasks	Suggested activities

3. May awaken during night crying (associated with wetting bed)
4. As he becomes more able to move about, he may uncover himself, become cold, and awaken

2. Check to see that child is covered
3. Avoid hazardous devices to keep child covered, including blanket clips, pins, and garments that enclose child to neck

19 to 30 months

1. Night: 10 to 12 hours
2. Naps: one (1 to 3 hours in duration)
3. Doesn't go to sleep at once—keeps demanding things
4. May awaken crying if wet or soiled
5. May awaken because of environmental change of temperature, change of bed, change of sleeping room, addition of sibling to room, absence of parent from home, hospitalization, trip with family, or relatives visiting

1. Quiet period of socialization prior to bedtime—reading child book or telling story
2. Holding child—talking quietly with him
3. Ritualistic behavior may be present; allow child to carry out routine; helps him overcome fear of unexpected or fear of dark; for example, child may wish to arrange toys in certain way
4. Explain bedtime ritual to baby-sitter
5. Give more reassurance, spend more time before bedtime preparation
6. Provide familiar bedtime toys or items
7. Allow crying-out period if he is safe, comfortable, and tucked in
8. Place in bed before he reaches excessive state of fatigue, excitement, or tiredness
9. Eliminate sources of stimulation or fear
10. Maintain consistent hour of bedtime

31 to 48 months

1. Daily range: 10 to 15 hours
2. Naps: beginning to disappear
3. Prolongs process of going to bed
4. Less dependent on taking toys to bed
5. May awaken crying from dreams
6. May awaken if wet

1. TV programs may affect ability to go to sleep; avoid violent TV programs
2. Anxiety about going to bed and desire to stay up with parents—requires limits
3. Regularity and consistency important to promote good sleeping habits
4. Reassurance—night light or leaving door ajar
5. Don't use bedtime or naptime as punishment
6. Encourage naps if signs of fatigue or irritability are evidenced

49 to 52 months

1. Daily range: 9 to 13 hours
2. Naps: rare
3. Quieter during sleep

1. Encourage napping if excessive or strenuous activity occurs and child is overly tired
2. Explain to child if sitter will be there after child is asleep

PLAY

Expected tasks	Suggested activities

1 to 3 months

1. Quieted when picked up
2. Regards face of others

1. Encourage holding and touching of child by mother
2. Provide with cradle gyms and mobiles, brightly colored, visually interesting objects within arm's distance

4 to 8 months

1. Plays with own body
2. Differentiates strangers from family
3. Seeks out objects
4. Grasps, holds, and manipulates objects
5. Repeats activities he enjoys
6. Bangs toys or objects together

1. Begin patty-cake and peek-a-boo
2. Provide for periods of solitary play (play-pen)
3. Encourage holding and touching of child by mother
4. Provide variety of multicolored and multitextured objects that child can hold
5. Encourage exploration of body parts
6. Provide floating toys for bath

9 to 12 months

1. Puts objects in and out of containers
2. Examines objects held in hand
3. Plays interactive games (peek-a-boo)
4. Extends toy to other person without releasing
5. Works to get toy out of reach

1. Continue mother-infant games
2. Give opportunity to place objects in containers and pour out
3. Provide large and small objects with which to play
4. Encourage interactive play

13 to 18 months

1. Plays by himself—may play near others
2. Has preferred toys
3. Enjoys walking activities, pulling toys
4. Throws and picks up objects, throws again
5. Imitates, i.e., reading newspaper, sweeping

1. Introduce to other children even though child may not play with them
2. Provide music, books, and magazines
3. Encourage imitative activities—helping with dusting, sweeping, stirring

19 to 30 months

1. Parallel play—not interactive but plays alongside another child
2. Uses both large and small toys
3. Rough-and-tumble play
4. Play periods longer than before—interested in manipulative and constructive toys
5. Enjoys rhymes and singing (TV programs)

1. Provide with new materials for manipulating and feeling—finger paints, clay, sand, stones, water, and soap
   Wooden toys—cars and animals
   Building blocks of various sizes, crayons, and paper
   Rhythmical tunes and equipment—swing, rocking chair, rocking horse
   Children's books—short, simple stories with repetition and familiar objects;

Expected tasks	Suggested activities
	enjoys simple pictures, brightly colored
	2. Guide child's hand to actively participate with specific activities, i.e., using crayons, hammering, etc.

31 to 48 months

Expected tasks	Suggested activities
1. In playing with others, beginning to interact, sharing toys, taking turns	1. Encourage play with small groups of children
2. Dramatizes, expresses imagination in play	2. Encourage imaginative and dramatic play activities
3. Combining playthings; more use of constructive materials	3. Music: singing and experimenting with musical instruments
4. Prefers 2 or 3 children to play with; may have special friend	4. Group participation in rhymes, dancing by hopping or jumping
	5. Drawing and painting (seldom recognizable)

49 to 52 months

Expected tasks	Suggested activities
1. Dramatic play and interest in going on excursions	1. Painting and drawing (objects will be out of proportion; details that are most important to child are drawn largest)
2. Fond of cutting and pasting, creative materials	2. Encourage printing of numbers and letters
3. Completes most activities	3. Clay: making recognizable objects
	4. Cutting and pasting
	5. Provide with materials for building sturdy structures with boxes, chairs, barrels, etc.

LANGUAGE

Expected tasks	Suggested activities

1 to 3 months

Receptive abilities

Expected tasks	Suggested activities
1. Movement of eyes, respiration rate, or body activity changes when bell is rung close to child's head	1. Observe facial expressions, gestures, bodily postures, and movements when vocalizations are being produced
2. Smiles when socially stimulated	2. Smile and talk softly in pleasant tone while holding, touching, and handling infant
3. Has facial, vocal, and generalized bodily responses to faces	3. Hold, touch, and interact frequently with infant for pleasure
4. Reacts differentially to adult voices	4. Refrain from letting infant engage in prolonged and incessant crying

Expressive abilities

1. Makes prelanguage vocalizations that consist of cooing, throaty sounds, e.g., gu
2. Makes "pleasure" sounds that consist of soft vowels

LANGUAGE–cont'd

Expected tasks	**Suggested activities**

1-3 months–cont'd

3. Makes "sucking" sounds
4. Crying can be differentiated for discomfort, pain, and hunger as reported by mother
5. An "A" sound as in cat is commonly heard in distress crying

4 to 8 months

1. Eyes locate source of sound
2. Responds to "hi, there" by looking up at face that is across and in front of him
3. Head turns to sound of cellophane held and crunched two feet away and at a 135-degree angle on either side of head
4. Will turn head to locate sound of "look here" when spoken at a 90-degree angle from head 2 feet away*
5. Turns head to sound of rattle
6. Responds differentially to vacuum cleaner, phone, doorbell, or sound of dog barking: may cry, whimper, look toward sound, or mother may report change in body tension
7. Responds by raising arms when mother reaches toward child and says "come up"

Expressive abilities
1. Uses different inflectional patterns:
   ah   uh   ah
2. Laughs aloud when stimulated
3. Has differential patterns of crying when hungry, in pain, or angry
4. Produces vowel sounds and chained syllables (baba, gugu, didi)
5. Makes "talking sounds" in response to others talking to him
6. Babbles to produce consonant sounds: ba, da, m-m
7. Vocalizes to toys
8. Says "da-da" or "ma-ma" but not specific to presence of parents

1. Engage in smiling eye-to-eye contact while talking to infant
2. Vocalize in response to inflectional patterns and when infant is producing babbling sounds; echo the sounds he makes
3. Observe for subtle communication clues such as eye aversion, struggling to move away, flushing of skin, tension of body, or movement of arms
4. Vocalize with infant during handling, while feeding, bathing, dressing, diapering, bedtime preparation, and holding
5. Stimulate laughing by light tickling
6. Observe child's reactions to bells, whistles, horns, phones, laughing, singing, talking, music box, noisemaking toys, and common household noises
7. While talking to infant, hold in position so that he can see your face
8. Have infant placed at position of eye level while talking to him throughout day
9. If crying or laughing sounds are not discerned at this stage, report to family physician, pediatrician, public health nurse, or well-child clinic

9 to 12 months

Receptive abilities
1. Ceases activity when name is pronounced or "no-no" is said

1. Gain child's attention when giving simple commands

---

*Do not test for localization of sound by producing sound directly behind infant's head.

Expected tasks	Suggested activities

2. Gives toys on request when accompanied by facial and bodily gestures
3. Attends to simple commands

Expressive abilities

1. Imitates definite speech sounds such as tongue clicking, lip smacking, or coughing
2. Should have two words that are *specific* for parents: "mama," "dada," or equivalents

2. Accompany oral directions with gestures
3. Vocalize with child during feeding, bathing, and playtimes
4. Provide sounds that child can reproduce such as lip smacking and tongue clicking
5. Repeat directions frequently and have child participate in action: open and close the drawer; move arms and legs up and down
6. Have child respond to verbal directions: stand up, sit down, close door, open door, turn around, come here

13 to 18 months

Receptive abilities

1. Attends to person speaking to child
2. Finds "the baby" in picture when requested, e.g., on baby food jar, in magazine, or in storybooks
3. Indicates wants by gestures
4. Looks toward family members or pets when named

Expressive abilities

1. Uses three words other than mama and dada to denote *specific* objects, persons, or actions
2. Indicates wants by naming object such as cookie

1. Incorporate repetition into daily routine of home
   a. Feeding: name baby's food and eating utensils; ask if he is enjoying his dessert; concentrate on reviewing day's events in simple manner
   b. Household duties: mother names each item as she dusts; pronounces word while cooking and preparing foods
   c. Playing: identify toys when using them; explain their function
2. Let child see mouthing of words
3. Encourage verbalization and expression of wants

19 to 30 months

Receptive abilities

1. Points to one named body part
2. Follows two or three verbal directions that are not accompanied by facial or body gestures, e.g., put ball on table, give it to mommy, or put toy in box

Expressive abilities

1. Combines two different words, e.g., "play ball," "want cookie"
2. Names object in picture, e.g., cat, bird, dog, horse, man
3. Refers to self by pronoun rather than by name

1. Continue to present concrete objects with words; talk about activities child is involved with
2. Include child in conversations during mealtimes
3. Encourage speech by having child express wants
4. Incorporate games into bathing routine by having child name and point to body parts
5. As child gains confidence in remembering and using words appropriately, encourage less use of gestures
6. Count and name articles of clothing as they are placed on child
7. Count and name silverware as it is placed on table

LANGUAGE–cont'd

Expected tasks	Suggested activities

19-30 months–cont'd

8. Sort, match, and name glassware, laundry, cans, vegetables, and fruit with child
9. Have child keep scrapbook and add new picture every day to increase recognition of vocabulary words
10. Spend 15 to 20 minutes per day going through booklets and naming pictures; have child point to pictures as objects are named
11. Help child develop functional core vocabulary to express safety needs and information about neighborhood
12. Whenever possible, use word (for example, paper), show object, have child handle and use it, encourage him to watch your face while you say the words, and suggest that he repeat it; refrain from undue pressure

31 to 36 months

Receptive abilities
1. Takes turns when asked while playing, eating, etc.
2. Attends longer to stories and TV programs
3. Demonstrates understanding of two prepositions by carrying out two commands one at a time, e.g., "put the block under the chair"
4. Can follow commands asking for two objects or two actions
5. Demonstrates understanding of concepts of big and little, e.g., selects larger of two balls when asked for big one
6. Points to additional body parts

Expressive abilities
1. Uses regular plurals, e.g., adds "s" to apple, box, orange (does not use irregular plurals, e.g., mouse to mice)
2. Gives first and last name
3. Names what he has drawn after scribbling
4. On request, tells you his sex, e.g., are you a little boy or a little girl?

1. Read stories with familiar content but with more detail: nonsense rhymes, humorous stories
2. Expect child to follow simple commands
3. Give child opportunity to hear and repeat his full name
4. Listen to child's explanation about pictures he draws
5. Encourage child to repeat nursery rhymes by himself and with others
6. Address child by his first name

Expected tasks	Suggested activities

5. Can repeat a few rhymes or songs
6. On request, tells what action is going on in picture, e.g., the kitten is eating

37 to 48 months

Expected tasks	Suggested activities
1. Expresses appropriate responses when asked what child does when tired, cold, or hungry	1. Provide visual stimuli while reading stories
2. Tells stories	2. Have child repeat story
3. Common expression: I don't know	3. Arrange trips to zoo, farms, seashore, stores, and movies and discuss with child
4. Repeats sentence composed of twelve to thirteen syllables, e.g., I am going when daddy and I are finished playing"	4. Give simple explanations in answering questions
5. Has mastered phonetic sounds of p, k, g, v, tf, d, z, lr, hw, j, kw, l, e, w, qe, and o	

49 to 52 months

Receptive abilities
1. Points to penny, nickel, or dime on request
2. Carries out in order command containing three parts, e.g., "pick up the block, put it on the table, and bring the book to me"

Expressive abilities
1. Names penny, nickel, or dime on request
2. Replies appropriately to questions such as, "What do you do when you are asleep?"
3. Counts three objects, pointing to each in turn
4. Defines simple words, e.g., hat, ball
5. Asks questions
6. Can identify or name four colors

Suggested activities
1. Play games in which child names colors
2. Encourage use of please and thank you
3. Encourage social-verbal interactions with other children
4. Encourage correct usage of words
5. Provide puppets or toys with movable parts that child can converse about
6. Provide group activity for child; children may stimulate each other by taking turns naming pictures
7. Allow child to make choices about games, stories, and activities
8. Have child dramatize simple stories
9. Provide child with piggy bank and encourage naming coins as they are handled or dropped into bank

DISCIPLINE

Expected tasks	Suggested activities

1 to 3 months

Expected tasks	Suggested activities
1. Draws attention by crying	1. a. Needs should be identified and met as promptly as possible
	b. Every bit of fussing should not be interpreted as emergency requiring immediate attention
	c. Infant should not be ignored and permitted to cry for exhaustive periods
2. Infant desires whatever is pleasant and wishes to avoid unpleasant situations	2. Begin to present limit of having to wait so that infant can learn that tension and

DISCIPLINE—cont'd

Expected tasks	Suggested activities

1-3 months—cont'd

	discomfort are bearable for short periods
3. Beginning to "wiggle" around	3. Place infant on surfaces that have sides to protect him from falling off

4 to 8 months

Expected tasks	Suggested activities
1. Begins to respond to "no-no"	1. a. Reserve "no-no" for times when it is really needed
	b. Be consistent with word "no-no" for same activity and event that requires it; be friendly and firm with verbal control of limit setting
2. Infant who is left alone for long periods of time may become bored or fretful; learns that crying and whining result in attention	2. Make special efforts to attend to infant when he is quiet and amusing himself
3. Beginning to show signs of timidity and fretfulness and may whimper and cry when mother separates from him or when strangers pick him up	3. a. Gradually introduce strangers into infant's environment
	b. Refrain from promoting frightening situations with strangers during this stage
	c. Play hiding games like peek-a-boo in which mother disappears and reappears
	d. Allow infant to cling to mother and get used to persons a little at a time
	e. If baby-sitter is used, find person familiar to infant or introduce for brief periods before mother leaves infant in her care
	f. Encourage gentle handling by mother, father, and siblings. Discourage rough handling, particularly by strangers
	4. a. Provide toys that do not have small detachable parts
4. Beginning to grasp objects and bring to mouth, but unable to differentiate safe from hazardous items	b. Check frequently for small objects in his line of reach
	5. When traveling in car, place in crib or seat with safety belts securely fastened

9 to 12 months

Expected tasks	Suggested activities
1. Beginning to respond to simple commands, e.g., "pick up the ball, put the toy in the box"	1. a. Avoid setting unreasonable number of limits
	b. Give simple commands one at a time
	c. Once limit is set, adhere to it firmly each time and connect it immediately with misbehavior

Expected tasks	Suggested activities
	d. Respond with consistency in enforcing rule
	e. Allow time to conform to request
	f. Gain child's attention
2. Ready to go places on his own and is trying out newly developing motor capacities (not to be confused with naughtiness, "spoiled," or stubbornness)	2. a. Begin setting and enforcing limits on where child is allowed to travel and explore
	b. Remove tempting objects
	c. Remove sources of danger such as light sockets, protruding pot handles, hanging table covers, sharp objects, and hanging cords
	d. Keep child away from fans, heaters, and certain drawers and don't place vaporizer close to infant's crib
	e. Keep highchair at least two feet away from working and cooking surfaces in kitchen
	f. Use gate to keep child out of kitchen when it is being used
	g. Be certain that pans, basins, and tubs of hot water are never left unattended
	h. Remove all possible poisons or substances that are not food that can be eaten or drunk off floor, low-level cabinets, and under sink
	i. Keep child from objects or surfaces that he may chew, e.g., porch rails, windowsills, *repainted* toys or cribs that may contain lead
	j. Instruct baby-sitter on all safety items
3. Has emerging desires to look at, handle, and touch objects	3. a. Experiment with diversionary measures
	b. Provide child with own play objects
4. Explores objects by sucking, chewing, and biting	4. a. Remove household poisons, cosmetics, pins, and buttons that he could put in his mouth
	b. Be certain that objects that go into mouth are hygienic
	c. Check toys for detachable small parts
5. Beginning to test reactions to certain parental responses during feeding and may become choosy about food	5. a. Once problem behaviors are defined, plan to work on changing only one behavior at a time until child behaves or conforms to expectations
	b. Be certain that child understands old rules before adding new ones

DISCIPLINE–cont'd

Expected tasks	Suggested activities

9-12 months–cont'd

	c.	Respond with consistency in enforcing old rules: enforce each time, don't ignore next time
	d.	Provide regular pattern of mealtimes
	e.	Refrain from feeding throughout day
	f.	Allow child to decide what he will eat and how much
	g.	Introduce new foods gradually over period of time
	h.	Continue to offer foods that may have been rejected first time
	i.	Don't force food
	j.	Refrain from physically punishing child for changes in eating habits
6. Beginning to test reactions to parental responses at bedtime preparation	6. a.	Provide regular time for naps and bedtime
	b.	Avoid excessive stimulation at bedtime or naptime
	c.	Ignore fussing and crying once safety and physical needs are satisfied and usual ritual is carried out
	d.	Keep child in own room
	e.	Refrain from picking up and rocking and holding if needs seem satisfied

13 to 18 months

1. Understands simple commands and requests	1. a.	Begin with one rule; add new ones as appropriate
	b.	In selecting new rules, choose on the basis of being able to clearly define it to self and child, having it reasonable and enforceable at all times; demand no more than fulfillment of defined expectations
	c.	Plan decisive limits and plan to give consistent attention to them
2. In learning mastery over impulses and self-control, child begins testing out limit setting	2. a.	Immediately correct errors in behavior as they occur
	b.	Use consistent enforcement of short-term rules (which are given as verbal commands) and long-term rules (which pertain to chores and family routines)

Expected tasks	Suggested activities
	c. Ignore temper tantrums
	d. Show child when you approve of his behavior and praise for obedience throughout day
3. With increasing fine motor control, child can manipulate objects that may be hazardous	3. a. Set limits regarding play with doorknobs and car door handles
	b. Keep away from open windows; latch screens
	c. Supervise around pools and ponds or drain or fence them
	d. Lock cabinets
	e. Keep open jars and bottles out of reach
	f. Use gate to protect child from falling down stairs

19 to 30 months

1. Attention span increasing	1. a. Gain attention before giving simple commands, one at a time; praise for success
	b. Add new rules as child conforms to old ones
	c. Refrain from expecting *immediate* obedience
2. Begins simple reasoning—asks question why; may be repetitive	2. Make special efforts to answer questions; give simple explanations; gauge need for simplicity by number of times act is repeated or question asked
3. Interested in further exploration of environment; may lack physical control	3. a. Supervise on stair rails and waxed floors
	b. Set rules about crossing streets and carrying knives, sharp objects, or glass objects
	c. Have outdoor play area securely fenced or supervised
	d. When riding in car, secure child safely by seat belt or insist on his sitting in back seat; do not permit standing on car seats
	e. Keep matches out of reach
	f. Shield adult tools such as knives, lawnmowers, sharp tools
4. Negativistic behavior is expected; responds more frequently with word "no"; may show more resistance at bedtime preparation and during mealtime	4. a. Practice consistency in responding to behavior
	b. Allow more time to conform to expectation
5. Behavior may change if new sibling is introduced into family unit	5. a. Explain verbally or through play that new child is expected
	b. Exercise more patience with child

DISCIPLINE—cont'd

Expected tasks	Suggested activities

19-30 months—cont'd

    c. Set special times aside for parental attention to child

    d. Allow child to help with special care tasks of new sibling

31 to 48 months

1. Displays more interest in conforming

  1. a. Exercise consistency in parental demands; enforce each time and avoid ignoring behavior next time

     b. Show concrete approval and give immediate recognition for acceptable behavior

     c. Refrain from use of threats that produce fearfulness

2. Shows greater understanding when simple reasoning is communicated

  2. a. Give simple explanations; allow child chance to demonstrate understanding by talking about event, situation, or rule

     b. Eliminate unnecessary and impractical rules

     c. Refrain from constant verbal reprimands

     d. Denial of privileges should not be excessive or prolonged

3. Will respond to simple commands such as putting toys away

  3. a. Assign simple household tasks that child can carry out each day; show approval for performance and success

     b. Decide if child is capable of doing what is asked by observing him

     c. Determine how much time is necessary to complete a chore or activity before expecting maximum performance

4. Displays greater independence in general activities

  4. a. Be extra cautious about supervising riding tricycles in streets and watching for cars in driveways

     b. Don't permit dashing into street while playing

     c. Don't allow child to follow ball into street

     d. Areas under swings and slides should not be paved

     e. Provide an imitative model that child can copy, e.g., don't jaywalk

     f. Provide scissors that are blunt tipped

Expected tasks	Suggested activities

49 to 52 months

Expected tasks	Suggested activities
1. Can be given two or three assignments at one time; will carry out in order	1. Give more opportunities to be independent
2. Complies readily with reasonable, well-defined, and consistent requirements	2. Use simple explanations and reasoning
3. Understands reasoning	3. Ask child to define role if he disobeys
	4. Have child correct mistakes as they occur
	5. Don't use punishment without warnings
	6. Praise for successful performance
	7. Use gold stars on chart for rewards
	8. If leaving for social obligation, vacation, or visiting away from home, let child know
	9. Avoid making promises that can't be kept
	10. Avoid bribing, ridicule, shaming, teasing, inflicting pain, using unfavorable comparison with other children, and exhibition of behavior by parents they are trying to stop in child
	11. Remember that child may be imitating models of behavior set up by parents, brothers, sisters, a neighborhood child, or maybe a TV hero
	12. Recognize that there are stress periods in family or child's life that may result in changes in child's behavior including accidents, illness, moving into new neighborhood, separation from friends, death, divorce, and hospitalization of child or parents (be more patient with child's behavior, give more time to conform, show more approval for mastery of tasks, and exercise consistency in handling problems as they occur)

TOILET TRAINING

Expected tasks	Suggested activities

9 to 12 months

Expected tasks	Suggested activities
1. Beginning to show regular patterns in bladder and bowel elimination	1. Watch for clues that indicate child is wet or soiled
2. Has one to two stools daily	2. Be sure to change diapers when wet or soiled so that child begins to experience contrast between wetness and dryness
3. Interval of dryness does not exceed 1 to 2 hours	

TOILET TRAINING—cont'd

Expected tasks	Suggested activities

13 to 18 months

Expected tasks	Suggested activities
1. Will have bowel movement if put on toilet at approximate time 2. Indicates wet pants	1. Sit child on toilet or potty chair at regular intervals for short periods of time throughout day 2. Praise child for success 3. If potty chair is used, it should be located in bathroom 4. Training should be started when social disruptions are at minimum 5. Respond promptly to signals and clues of child by taking him to bathroom or changing pants 6. Use training pants, once toilet training is commenced 7. Plan to begin training when disruptions in regular routine are minimized, i.e., don't begin on vacation

19 to 30 months

Expected tasks	Suggested activities
1. Anticipates need to eliminate 2. Same word for both functions 3. Daytime control (occasional accident) 4. Requires assistance (reminding, dressing, wiping)	1. Continue regular intervals of toileting 2. Reward success 3. Dress in simple clothing that child can manage 4. Remind occasionally, particularly after mealtime, juicetime, naptime, and playtime 5. Take to bathroom before bedtime 6. Bathroom should be convenient to use, easy to open door

31 to 48 months

Expected tasks	Suggested activities
1. Takes responsibility for toilet if clothes are simple 2. Continues to verbalize need to go; apt to hold out too long 3. May have occasional accident 4. Needs help with wiping	1. May still need reminding 2. Dress in simple clothing that child can manage 3. Ignore accidents; refrain from shame or ridicule

49 to 52 months

Expected tasks	Suggested activities
1. General independence (anticipates needs, undresses, goes, wipes, washes hands)	1. Praise child for his accomplishment

DRESSING

Expected tasks	Suggested activities

13 to 18 months

Expected tasks	Suggested activities
1. Cooperates in dressing by extending arm or leg 2. Removes socks, hat, mittens, shoes	1. Encourage child to remove socks, etc. after task is initiated for him 2. Do not rush child

Expected tasks	Suggested activities
3. Can unzip zippers	3. Have him practice with large buttons and
4. Tries to put shoes on	with zippers

19 to 30 months

1. Can undress	1. Provide opportunities to button with extra-large–sized buttons
2. Can remove shoes if laces are untied	2. Encourage and allow opportunity for self-help in getting drink, removing clothes with help, hand washing, un-buttoning, etc.
3. Helps dress	
4. Tries to unbutton	3. Simple clothing
5. Pulls on simple clothes	4. Provide mirror at height child can observe himself for brushing teeth, etc.

31 to 48 months

1. Greater interest and ability in dressing	1. Provide with own dresser drawer
2. Intent on lacing shoes (usually does incorrectly)	2. Simple garments encourage self-help; do not rush child
3. Does not know back from front	3. Provide large buttons, zippers, slipover clothing
4. Washes and dries hands, brushes teeth	4. Self hand washing but help with brushing teeth
5. Can button	5. Provide regular routine for dressing, either in bathroom or bedroom

49 to 52 months

1. Dresses and undresses with care except for tying shoes and buckling belts	1. Assign regular task of placing clothes in hamper or basket
2. May learn to tie shoes	2. Continue to use simple clothing
3. Combs hair with assistance	3. Encourage self-help in dressing and un-dressing
	4. Allow child to select clothes he will wear

CASE ILLUSTRATION

The following case illustration represents an approach to summarizing significant observations about the child, his functioning, and the parents' practices. This format has been helpful to nurses in reporting their findings when using the *Washington Guide.*

CLINICAL RECORD

Sam Smith

Date: 12/3　　　　　　　　　　Chronological Age: 5 years 8 months

Nursing assessment

This follow-up home visit was made for the purpose of determining Sam's current levels of functioning in self-help skills and play.

An application of the *Washington Guide* revealed the following profile:

ASSESSMENT OF FUNCTIONAL ABILITIES

Motor development: Motor tasks fall within the range of 9 to 12 months of age (able to stand momentarily, walk with support [holding onto furniture], and pick up a raisin with right thumb and finger).

Language: Receptive and expressive abilities appear to be at the low end of the 4- to 8-month scale. His head turns when a bell is rung and when others talk to him. He responds by raising arms when parents request him to come near or up. Expressive abilities include laughing aloud and emitting vowel sounds. No words were elicited.

Play behaviors: Play activities range within a 4- to 8-month level of development. He amuses himself for short intervals. He presently lacks initiative in spontaneously exploring his play environment, that is, toys are selected and presented to him. Play objects are held momentarily and released. The majority of toys presented to him are explored by mouth. Transparent objects are characteristically licked with lips and tongue, raised to eye level, and lowered again in stereotyped fashion, to be explored with mouthing movements. He engaged in sitting and pushing a musical ball back and forth with his father. Pushing, rather than holding, releasing, and tossing are characteristics of this particular activity. Imitative behaviors for scribbling with a crayon, dialing a toy phone, or hitting a pounding block with a toy hammer could not be elicited. Samples of problem-solving behaviors are absent.

Discipline: Responses are characteristic of a 4- to 8-month-old level of development. He occasionally responds to no-no.

Feeding skills: Presently he is functioning within a range of 9 to 12 months of age. He drinks from a cup with assistance, finger feeds, and is beginning to progress in independent feeding with a spoon.

Dressing skills: He falls below the 16-month norm for independently removing a garment. He does anticipate dressing by extending arms and legs, a 13-month-old task.

Toileting: He does not indicate needs, a 13- to 18-month-old developmental task.

This informal assessment provided the opportunity for acknowledging the parents' past and present efforts for giving Sam an appropriate environment for his present level of functional abilities, that is, their expectations for performance correspond readily to his abilities rather than his chronological age. He is provided with varied sources of sensory stimulation, opportunities to move about freely, and his parents are attempting to fulfill his emotional and social needs.

Behavioral observations: It has become more apparent that Sam has developed some effective behavioral patterns to gain parental attention. The parents responded immediately to a number of Sam's attention-seeking behaviors; for example, they responded to his arm waving and frequent whining by putting records on for Sam's benefit, turning the TV on, taking him downstairs to swing, walking him back and forth across the living room, and placing him in a rocker.

CHIEF CONCERN AS EXPRESSED BY MOTHER

Mrs. Smith asserted herself in the absence of Mr. Smith to express her desire for meeting and communicating with another mother who is confronted with the needs of a handicapped child. Appropriate arrangements for this request will be explored further in future contacts with the mother.

Recommendations

In consideration of this random sample of parent-child interactions and the lack of consistent and systematic limit setting by both parents, it would appear that the Smiths might benefit from exploring a method to modify their responses to these constant attention-seeking behaviors. Another priority to consider is the need for consistently gaining Sam's attention for any task or performance expected of him.

Specific programs for developmental stimulation will be suggested after further observations are collected. Additional observations should be made to determine the frequency of the child's attention-getting behaviors and the parents' responses to them.

Sara Dippity, R.N.

REFERENCES

Campbell, M. M., and Ramsey, O. E.: Developmental screening scales (composite of the Cattell Infant Scale, the Gesell Scales, the Composite Scale by B. M. Caldwell and R. H. Drachman's Scale, and the Vineland Social Maturity Scale), Seattle, 1965, Clinic for Child Study, University of Washington (mimeographed).

Dittmann, L. L.: The nurse in home training programs for the retarded child, Social Security Administration and Children's Bureau, U. S. Department of Health, Education, and Welfare, Washington, D. C., 1961, U. S. Government Printing Office.

Dittmann, L. L.: The mentally retarded child at home: a manual for parents, Welfare Administration and Children's Bureau, U. S. Department of Health, Education, and Welfare, Washington, D. C., 1964, U. S. Government Printing Office.

Doll, E. A.: Vineland social maturity scale: manual of directions, Minneapolis, 1947, Educational Test Bureau, Educational Publishers, Inc.

Frankenburg, W. K., and Dodds, J. B.: Denver developmental screening test, Denver, Ladoca Project and Publishing Foundation.

Gesell, A., and Ilg, F. L.: Feeding behavior of infants, Philadelphia, 1937, J. B. Lippincott Co.

Gesell, A.: The first five years of life: A guide to the study of the pre-school child, New York, 1940, Harper and Brothers, Publishers.

Ginott, H. G.: Between parent and child: new solutions to old problems, New York, 1969, Avon Books.

Hedrick, D., and Prather, E., chief investigators: Washington language scale, Seattle, 1970, University of Washington Child Development and Mental Retardation Center.

Holtgrewe, M. M.: A guide for public health nurses working with mentally retarded children, Welfare Administration and Children's Bureau, U. S. Department of Health, Education, and Welfare, Washington, D. C., 1964, U. S. Government Printing Office.

Illingworth, R. S.: The normal child: some problems of the first five years and their treatment, Boston, 1964, Little, Brown & Co.

Jensen, G. D.: The well child's problems: management in the first six years, Chicago, 1962, Year Book Medical Publishers, Inc.

Paulus, A. C.: A tool for the assessment of the retarded child at home, Nursing Clinics of North America, Philadelphia, December, 1966, W. B. Saunders Co.

Spock, B.: Baby and child care, New York, 1957, Pocket Books, Inc.

6
Observation of the environment and behavior

Professionals in the field of mental retardation are faced with the task of coming to some solution regarding simple as well as complex problems of children and their families. These may include self-help skills, peer interactions, activity levels, attention to tasks, and responses to limit setting, to name a few.

As part of the assessment process, nurses generally have the choices of seeing the child, taking a history, making a home visit, and discussing the problem with parents, siblings, or colleagues.

If the nurse elects to see the child in the home or other setting, what does she really look for and at? Often she sees a number of complex factors that must be explored in an in-depth, systematic way.

If she discusses the problem with the parent or teacher, does she rely solely on what information is conveyed to her? It is advisable that she remain cautious about reaching conclusions based on subjective interpretations of others' reports. If she has the time, responsibility, and confidence of identifying and intervening in a problem, where does she begin? In attempting to pinpoint a concern, generally all nurses experience the frustration of not having enough information, hearing stereotyped conclusions of why the child is behaving in a certain way, listening to subjective descriptions of a problem based on personal bias, or dealing with a lack of specific up-to-date information on a child's behavior. Maybe the nurse has information only on how a child is reacting in one situation and not in another. Too often we have a tendency first of all to gain quickly an impression of what we think is wrong and try something out only to find it does not work immediately. Then we try something else without completing a series of systematic observations and end up with unsuccessful solutions.

Sometimes nurses listen to parents and give advice on different ways to handle a problem of concern, only to find that the parent is dismayed again with failure and possibly feels more guilty than ever and more inadequate in not being able to cope successfully with the situation.

COLLECTION OF BEHAVIORAL DATA

Nurses are now using new approaches to old problems. One-shot observations of behavior in reaching clinical diagnoses have been gotten away from; instead, the emphasis is being placed on serial, ongoing observations over a period of time under different conditions. More supporting evidence and accurate data are being used before intervening in the management of problems, whether they are nutritional, academic, problems in the self-help skills, or behavioral problems. The need to have a clear picture before giving counsel to parents is acknowledged. Nurses are becoming much more sensitive to the deficits in information they receive if a problem is referred. Without question, nurses are becoming convinced of the need to have a really in-depth picture of a problem confronting a parent or a child.

In doing a better job, nurses are beginning to rely more on systematic methods rather than intuitive judgement. In making a total behavioral assessment of an individual, it becomes crucial to become accustomed to and oriented toward counting and recording behaviors.

WHAT TO OBSERVE

If a mother describes her child as always having a temper tantrum, the topography of this behavior has to be examined. In other words, when does the child start fussing or whimpering, when does crying begin, do the pitch and tone accelerate, does the crying go on for longer periods of time, when does crying usually occur, and what behavioral responses are generated by others if crying does happen? Reports from persons taking care of a child often tend to be biased. For example, a mother may report her child as stubborn. The mother could help objectify the picture by actually counting the behaviors of concern. A mother, for instance, may report that her child always resists setting the dinner table, does not mow the lawn when asked, never maintains his bedroom and belongings, doesn't care adequately for his pet, and won't wash the dishes or take out the garbage. What might be important here is to determine within a given time limit the precise number of times the child did complete his household chores and the amount of time spent in a given activity during the week. If the mother reports a problem of sibling rivalry, it might be advantageous to find out by counting and recording how often one child takes a toy away from another, how often a child cries in the presence of a sibling or clings to his mother, what established behavoirs are changing, how often he wets or exhibits less mature behaviors, that is, "regresses," and how much time his mother spends with him alone.

Attention-seeking behavior

How much attention a child seems to want and seems to get from others can be roughly gauged by noting what he does to get attention and how often he does it. Attention getting may take the form of making more verbal noises, crying, whining, screaming, pulling, clinging, and touching. The child may draw attention to himself through object manipulation—getting into food on a shelf, knocking a dish to the floor, or dropping something. He may take a toy away from his brother or sister or hit or strike them. The child may engage in some form of stimulatory behavior like rocking, hitting his head, or masturbation. He may go near places he knows to be "off limits." The nurse should observe how a child is behaving when the mother is not near, how a child acts to gain his mother's attention, and how the parent responds to the child's cues. It should be noted when the specific response from the child occurred, how often it occurred, and how effective it was in producing the desired result.

Communication patterns

The nurse should try to determine the nature and effectiveness of the child's communication with his family. He may communicate by pointing, touching, or pulling. His wishes may be anticipated and indulged with no attempt made to encourage verbal effort. The frequency and the usual circumstances under which the child is spoken to should be noted, as well as whether or not family members reinforce the child's verbal efforts by paying attention to what he says. It is important to find out about the manner in which the family attempts to communicate with the child. Do they put their questions and requests simply and slowly, or do they string out a long, complex combination of words that has to be repeated? If the mother reports that "he understands what I say to him," it is important to observe how many times a request has to be given and how soon the child responds. Does he respond immediately, soon after, or not at all until the request is repeated?

Physical contact

The nurse should describe situations of parent-child contact and how and when parents demonstrate their affection to the child. While talking to the mother about the child, the nurse can be aware of signs of hostility, overprotection, rejection, or discomfort in the relationship. For example, many mothers report that they use punishment excessively because they have not found other ways to control negative behavior. One possible effect is that the child comes to expect punishment and failure as inevitable in his life. Often parents need to be reoriented to seeing what is positive in the child's behavior and reacting accordingly.

Some other points to check are as follows:
1. How do the parents let the child know he has pleased them?
2. Do they get the child's attention before trying to teach him?
3. Do the parents give clues, specific directions, or demonstrations when teaching a task?
4. Do the tasks they are teaching him seem appropriate?

PLANNING THE OBSERVATION

To observe actual situations in regard to child management, it is generally best to plan your visit for a time when some natural interaction goes on, such as mealtime or when the child is being prepared for a nap or being dressed. You might also ask the parent to set up some situations by getting the child to do a task, stop misbehavior, or demonstrate rules that have been established.

Others who are significant in a child's life may offer descriptions of a child's behavior. A frustrated preschool teacher might report that a child "has a poor attitude." She may describe the child as always out of his seat, usually talking out of turn, constantly making inappropriate noises in the classroom, and never following instructions. What is important here is to gain some objective observations on the number of times the child repositions himself somewhere else in the room, how many times he is observed to be out of his seat, and how soon he follows instructions once given.

By using observational skills and behavioral records, the task of assessment becomes easier, since one has precise descriptions and quantification of behaviors. Often failure with preacademic problems is blamed on "a short attention span." Rather than be satisfied with such a description from a parent, another nurse, physician, or preschool teacher, the nurse making an assessment can keep track of and record the time that the child spent engaged in looking or was involved with a particular task, toy, event, or another child. This becomes crucial in establishing a base line of behaviors and assists in the accurate and appropriate planning for methods that might sustain the child's attention.

Another example in which counting behaviors is crucial is in the area of infant stimulation. What is actually important to know is how many times an infant is repositioned in his crib, how many toys he has in his room, what sizes and shapes these toys are, how many different colors there are, and how often this child plays with his toys and for what length of time. What positions is this child held in during the day; for instance, is he placed on the floor all day long or is he moved to different heights? How many times is he moved from one height to another? How many times is he spoken to? What is the content of the language that he hears? How much eye contact does he get from his caretakers? How frequently does he have tactile stimulation? How much variety is there in the textures of toys that he plays with; for example, does he have the opportunity to play with smooth, rough, soft, hard, bright, and dull toys? In the area of verbal stimulation, it is important to know who talks to him, how often, how many words are said, what his responses are, how many times he coos, how many times he babbles in response to what is said to him, and how many caretakers he interacts with during a given day.

The purpose of recording observations in a systematic way is that the accuracy of data about a problem can often lead to more sound bases for nursing intervention. There may be a tendency for all observations to be influenced by beliefs created by our own past experience, reports from others, our own predetermined expectations, and our own perceptual sets. In making a total behavioral assessment of a child, one should note carefully the quantity of behaviors under consideration.

RECORDING THE OBSERVATION

Behavioral recordings customarily begin with a narrative account of the sequences of an individual's behavior. A narrative account is a preliminary procedure to obtain a general impression of the behaviors. The recording of narrative written accounts should be continued until there is satisfaction that the principal problem behavior can be categorized into observable units. It is useful to convert a narrative account into a three-column table to help gain a more precise picture or impression of the relationships among antecedent events, responses, and consequences of selected behaviors. Illustrations of a narrative, three-column recording and a tally are given.

Narrative record of a preschool child described as "hyperactive" by parents, physician, and kindergarten teacher

Observation time: ten minutes
Setting: Kindergarten classroom
Example of narrative:

L. is standing near teacher in classroom with arms outstretched saying "dough, dough" twenty-three times. Grabs and pushes carriage toward and into cabinet. Walks backward pulling carriage. Teacher approaches. L. leans over carriage and touches cover. Goes to sandbox and back to carriage. Picks up cover, shakes twice, and drops cloth to floor. Lifts, shakes, and covers doll and moves carriage back and forth. Moves carriage toward blackboard, pulls it back, and leaves it in center of room. L. goes toward sandbox. Walks away from sandbox and goes to play table. Rubs both hands over flour and surface of table. Teacher instructs L. to "come here." L. rushes past teacher and out of view. L. is next seen touching the handle of the carriage with one hand, then places feet inside, sits down, and looks straight ahead. He climbs out and pulls carriage near the sandbox area. L. kneels down and moves the legs of the doll inside the carriage. Goes to sandbox, looks at another child, picks up container, moves it, and looks up at teacher. Teacher drops sand into a container. L. watches, moves, and pours sand into container three times. Teacher places and ties apron from behind. L. pours sand three times. Teacher approaches and demonstrates how the sand wheel turns. L. leaves and places himself prone on play steps, gets up, lifts, lies, and crawls over the steps. He stands and then walks away while teacher demonstrates turning over the boat. L. goes to table, sits, gets up, looks around, moves around table, picks up an object, and runs toward carriage. Pulls carriage backwards and leaves it next to sand table. Walks to sand table, picks up a pouring container, drops it and walks away, and points outdoors. L. goes toward window, stands, looks out, and moves to the right. Sees Playskool, picks it up, places it on floor, looks up at teachers, and places circular objects in Playskool. Teacher approaches, L. continues to play, and teacher demonstrates activity of placing objects inside the box.

Three-column table for recording behavioral events

Time	Antecedent event	Responses	Consequent social event
9:30	Child receives instruction to find Play Dough from teacher	Goes to table, sits, and begins touching play dough	Teacher praises student for sitting quietly and playing

Use of a tally

Once a discrete behavior has been observed and records are necessary to note the frequency of its occurrence, a tally can be used to obtain a frequency account during a specified time interval. When an individual initiates or engages in a specified behavior, the observer marks the incidence of the response and adds the total number. An example of a tally for recording frequency of behaviors follows.

Behavior during this observation period is defined as any gross motor activity that involves touching, moving toward, moving away from, actively moving, removing, replacing, lifting, lowering, manipulating, shaking, pushing, pulling, rubbing, opening, closing, sitting on, standing on, or climbing in, out, or on any of the following objects.

Record separate actions only to determine the frequency of occurrence.

Carriage /XX/ /XX/ //
Cabinet /
Sandbox /XX/ /
Cloth cover /XX/
Rag doll /XX/
Window //
Play table /XX/ /

Flour /
Pouring container for sand /X/ /X/ /
Blackboard /
Sand wheel /
Play steps /X/
Boat /
Playskool ///
Circular objects /

Total <u>60</u>

From this point, the nurse would need to determine what behaviors are being emitted at the highest rate. It would be important to determine also what behaviors are being produced at the lowest rate. The decision would then be made about what other behavior samples to get in order to pinpoint an area of concern for intervention.

PURPOSE OF RECORDING

The purposes of recording observations in a systematic way are as follows:

1. To establish the duration or frequency of a specified behavior
2. To clearly and accurately define a problem of concern
3. To determine the relationships between behaviors and the consequences they produce
4. To differentiate nonobservable behaviors from those that can be seen, counted, and recorded
5. To determine priorities of concern
6. To establish a base line for planning certain interventions
7. To evaluate the effectiveness of interventions

In addition to these purposes, the value of recording behavioral events as they occur has been found to be the following:

1. Once recording begins, whether by a teacher, a parent, or a nurse, all may more easily see some positive features of a child rather than the negative perceptions to which they are accustomed. In other words, we begin to look at assets and strengths of a child rather than just picking out the negative features.

2. A new perspective about a child can begin to emerge—those concerned, whether it be parents, teachers, or nurses, become more certain about what they prefer about a child's behavior and what they don't like.

3. Sometimes a negative cycle or network begins to change, just with observation alone.

4. Parents start to experience feeling less anger if asked to keep records. This may be a substitution for shouting at or administering punishment to a child.

5. Records can serve as indicators of how concerned parents really are and possibly how willing and committed they are to having a behavior change. A good example is in the area of toilet training, in which parents are asked to keep records. Whether they are making progress can be evaluated either by the fact that records are kept or not kept or by the progress that is being recorded by the person involved in the teaching.

6. Counting certain behaviors helps us determine what else we need to look for. For example, if a child does have a temper tantrum, what does the parent do? How does he respond? We need to examine adult behaviors as well. We need to record adult behaviors and tally them and monitor them along with the child's responses.

7. Surprisingly enough, a phenomenon occurs in that sometimes a problem doesn't really exist. As recorded evidence about the frequency of a "problem" behavior accumulates, it becomes apparent that the behavior is not as frequent as the parents originally thought.

OBSERVATION OF THE GENERAL ENVIRONMENT

An assessment of the child's general environment should be incorporated along with other observations of interactions. The child's environment should be examined and evaluated to determine its advantages or disadvantages for the child. In other words, what stimuli are lacking, what stimuli are excessive, and what stimuli should be altered? For instance, while you are observing the child, take note of the colors in the room. A bright, attractive, and interesting color scheme is to be favored over a drab, monotonous room because it presents a more stimulating, enjoyable visual experience. What play equipment is available that is appropriate for the child's stage of development? Can the child get at it easily? What toys does he prefer? What about outdoor space and privileges? Does the child play with others?

Colorful mobiles are especially good for the child whose environmental scope is limited because he is inactive or because he is confined to a small area. Such children are in special need of environmental stimuli. The level of perceptiveness of a child restricted to a crib many hours a day may be reduced. He sees so little going on about him that he does not develop the normal inclination to look around and explore.

What other forms of stimulation are there in the environment? Are auditory cues, such as voices and music, lacking? Are radios or television sets turned on throughout the day, providing only a monotonous low-level stimulus for the child?

Again, the quality of a child's environment can be determined by quantifying it, that is, counting the number of stimuli present or absent.

PLAY OBSERVATIONS

Like other children, the retarded child masters developmental tasks through play. Since play is a major occupation for children, its importance for observation and assessment is emphasized.

Just as there is a developmental sequence to language, there is also a developmental sequence to play, and children can be assessed according to the level they have reached in play. A detection of the child's developmental level of play is facilitated either by observing the child manipulating a toy or toys or through observations of the child interacting in play with siblings or his peers. For example, if the child is chronologically 5 years old and still has not acquired the skill of throwing a ball overhand, a nurse would make a judgment that there is a discrepancy when compared to normative standards and would automatically take a closer, more in-depth look at both the child's gross and fine motor development, the way he walks, his speech, and his general behavior.

While observing a child at play, a nurse should note his attention span to a given toy, his ability to use the toy in imitation, and his social responses when interacting with another. It may be that deficits in play behavior can signal the need for intervention, whereby attention is focused on building play behaviors so that the child can move to a more advanced level, which may influence advancement in other areas of his general development.

As with self-help skills or language, the goal in the area of play is to promote a more advanced level of play behavior for a child. The nurse should plan appropriate play activity suitable for a child's current development, as well as beginning preparation for the next appropriate level. It is important in planning a home visit to indicate to the mother that you will be bringing some selected toys that will be presented to her child in a play session.

SELECTED OBSERVATIONS

The added benefit of using toys is that it permits the nurse to make observations of other areas while the child is playing. Motor, social, and problem-solving abilities and the child's attention span are an integral part of play responses. Just as the behaviors that comprise self-help functions are subdivided, it is helpful to systematically and in detail analyze the component movements involved in both gross and fine motor activities. It is not enough to observe the arm movements a child makes when contacting a toy. Consideration is given to the observable fact that the child looks at, reaches, grasps, holds onto, explores, and makes releasing movements of the hand. In addition, close observation of the thumb and finger grasp can be noted when a child is playing with a smaller toy. How well a child uses his fingers is important to note while assessing fine motor skills. Present the child with large objects or toys initially, notice what he can do with his hands, arms, and fingers, and gradually present him with toys that require more refined manipulative behaviors. To determine the reach that an infant or child has, select dangling toys that stimulate this response. Present a rattle or toys with a handle that reveal the child's ability to hold an object in his palm.

Next in order is the presentation of a movable object or toy that can be pressed together or banged together, giving the observer clues to the child's eye-hand coordination. Two small sticks can be used to stimulate this response, as well as having the child do a patty-cake routine. Throwable toys like a ball are useful for indicating the child's abilities in manipulation and arm movement. Presenting the child with take-apart and stacking toys will determine the control the child has of his hands as he opens and closes them. With each presentation, take the opportunity of determining the child's ability to imitate manipulating the toy, if he does not spontaneously demonstrate appropriate behaviors. Imitative behaviors can always be capitalized on for teaching desired behaviors. As the nurse sequentially presents the child with toys, it is recommended that she increase her expectations of the child's performance by presenting toys that require more complex behavior. For instance, bead-stringing requires finger and thumb movement in combination rather than grasping with the palm. To determine how well the fingers function together or work independently, present such play items as a telephone to be dialed or a toy shoe to be laced. Drawing paper is useful to give the child an opportunity to crease and thus follow a simple request or to help the nurse determine the landmarks attained in the use of prewriting skills. If the child does not scribble spontaneously, do not necessarily expect him to draw a circle or square.

Always present the child with one object at a time, thus narrowing the stimuli to which he must attend. Secure the child's attention before expecting any performance and note again the small steps he may take in reaching the goal you have set for him. Acknowledge these steps by your own form of social recognition by praise or affectionate responses. Seek the highest, rather than the lowest, level in play as you would in other behaviors. At the same time that the nurse is observing behaviors that are occurring, she can be thinking about ways to further develop the potential the child currently exhibits in play. Again, she orients herself in planning ahead to the possibility of building new skills on the ones already unfolding.

Toys can therefore be used in the following ways while observing a child:

1. To get a child's attention
2. To determine the kinds of imitative behaviors he engages in

3. To gauge his tolerance for frustration
4. To evaluate the quality of his fine and gross motor skills
5. To assess his ability to stick with a task to completion
6. To observe his responsiveness to praise
7. To assess his problem-solving abilities
8. To note his general reactions to toys and whether they are appropriate
9. To determine the levels of interactions that he has while playing with others, either with toys or in games

We are also interested in knowing if a child exhibits a solitary, parallel, cooperative, or collaborative level of play and whether or not the child is exploring toys, whether toys elicit language responses in a child, and whether it helps him with his spatial relationships and his ability to discriminate differences such as colors, designs or shapes of toys. Through play as a focus, we can find out about the environment in which the child is learning to master his tasks. It is important to have information on whether or not there are toys available to the child in his environment. We need to know if he is permitted to use these toys and if they are selected according to his particular needs and responses. Are there appropriate playmates with whom the child can develop socializing skills? Are these children at his developmental level or are they older or younger? If his mother states that she plays with her child, is it a genuine form of play or is the child learning something academic under the guise of play as the mother interprets play? With the data gained from observing the child or by interpreting the reports we hear about the nature of a child's play, one can plan therapeutic goals with play as a focus. The nurse can use it to modify a child's behavior. She can prescribe specific exercises, games, or toys to enhance the child's gross motor coordination or to promote fine-skilled behaviors. She can counsel on the use of toys to increase a child's attention span; these would most likely be toys that are bright, attractive, and give pleasure in sensorimotor areas so that the child will repeat and possibly move on to the next level of not just attending to a toy, but exploring it and initiating movement with the toy or imitating how somebody else uses the toy. Play might be used as a means of increasing mothering behaviors with a child, which could not be accomplished in other ways. Maybe a mother needs guidance to realize that her child needs as much attention to play as he does to learning preacademic concepts or his self-help skills. A successful and nonthreatening play situation can create successful effects rather than another frustrating experience to a mother who may be experiencing a minimal amount of feedback from her child. It can be the launching place for mothers to learn realistic expectations and come to better developmental appraisals of their children.

REFERENCE

1. Harris, F. R., Allen, K. E., and Johnston, M. S.: Methodology for experimental studies of young children in natural settings, Psychol. Rec. **19:**177-210, 1969.

ADDITIONAL READINGS

Bijou, S. W., and Baer, D. M.: Child development: a systematic and empirical theory, vol. I, New York, 1961, Appleton-Century-Crofts.

Carbonara, N. T.: Techniques for observing normal child behavior, Pittsburgh, 1961, University of Pittsburgh Press.

Murphy, L. B.: Assessment of infants and young children. In Dittmann, L. L., editor: Early child care: the new perspectives, New York, 1968, Atherton Press.

section four
LEARNING TO LEARN

The decision to move in a particular direction to help a child develop his functional skills is shaped by the information that has been gathered on the child's developmental level, his interactions with his parents, the nature and effect of the environment, and whether the parents can recognize the possibilities of change and act on this recognition. The nurse then considers behavior that should be strengthened, weakened, or changed. The mother can be asked what she desires in terms of behavioral change. What does the child do that concerns her most? What is he lacking that is important to her?

The nurse then develops a plan that will help the child and his parents. The program should be neither insignificant nor excessively ambitious. It is not advisable to attempt changing too many forms of behavior at once. For example, if a mother says she wants her child to have good table manners and stop throwing his plate every night, the first steps in the plan should be toward putting a stop to plate throwing.

In planning with the parents for the work to be done with the child, small goals that lead to bigger accomplishments should be considered. The nurse should expect to make frequent home visits at first. They may be necessary for meeting some of the parents' dependency needs, for interpreting information received from evaluations, or for recording data on the child's behavior. During these first contacts the nurse can help the parents understand the goals to be accomplished and the fact that they themselves are going to learn how to help their child progress by applying principles of child development.

7
Motor skills

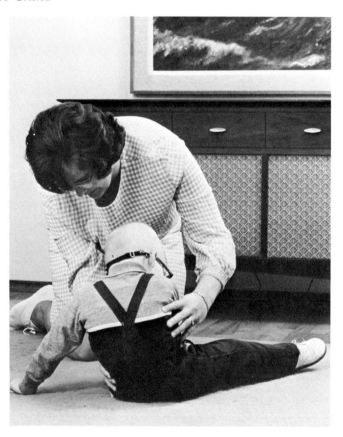

The basic building blocks of further development in learning and cognitive behavior depend on the child's motor skills, his ability to walk, and his ability to grasp and manipulate objects. Therefore it is extremely important that the nurse assess the child's ability to move around, to grasp things, and, if the child does not have age-appropriate skills in this area, to begin to develop the appropriate motor skills needed to enhance development. The refinement of motor skills is necessary for the mastery of other developmental tasks and self-help skills.

A composite of suggested activities to enhance motor skills from the *Washington Guide* is presented here.

SUGGESTED ACTIVITIES FOR ENHANCING MOTOR SKILLS

1 to 3 months
1. Place the infant in prone position.
2. Support him in sitting position with his head erect.
3. Pull infant to sitting position.
4. Provide with opportunity to observe people or activity.
5. Hand bright-colored objects and mobiles within reach across crib.
6. Provide with opportunity to observe objects or people while in sitting position.
7. Use infant seat.
8. Alternate bright, shiny objects with dark and light visual patterns.

4 to 8 months
1. Pull up to sitting position.
2. Provide opportunity to sit supported or alone when head and trunk control are stabilized.
3. Put bright-colored objects within reach.
4. Give toys or household objects: rattles, teething ring, cloth animals or dolls, 1-inch cubes, plastic objects such as cups, rings, or balls.
5. Offer small objects such as cereal to improve grasp.
6. Offer variety of patterns or textures to play with.
7. Use squeak toys.

9 to 12 months
1. Provide playpen, allow child to pull himself to standing position.
2. Give opportunity and space to practice creeping and crawling.
3. Have child practice moving on his knees to improve balance prior to walking.
4. Have child use walker or straddle toys.

5. Play airplane with child, have child practice catching himself while rolling on large ball.
6. Provide with objects such as spoons, plastic bottles, cups, ball, cubes, finger foods, saucepans, and lids.

13 to 18 months
1. Provide opportunity to practice walking and climbing stairs with help.
2. Give toys that can be pushed around.
3. Supervise activity with paper and large crayons.
4. Provide toys such as cubes, cups, saucepans, lids, rag dolls, and other soft, cuddly toys.
5. Begin introducing child to swing.

19 to 30 months
1. Provide opportunities to practice and develop activities.
2. Provide pattern for child while he watches and then encourage him to try.
3. Provide tricycle or similar pedal toys. Secure his foot on pedal if necessary.

31 to 48 months
1. Continue with blocks, combining materials, toy cars, and trains.
2. Provide clay and other manipulating materials.
3. Give opportunities to swing and climb.
4. Provide with activities such as finger painting, chalk, and blackboard.

49 to 52 months
1. Provide with music and games to synchronize hand and foot tapping with music, skipping, hopping, and dancing rhythmically to improve coordination.

These activities are arranged in relation to age. It is suggested that first the child's level of functioning be identified and then the skills listed be used as the basis for planning a program that will enable the child to develop the particular motor skills that he needs in a step-by-step course.

A program that was developed to enhance the development of sitting-up behavior in infants with delayed development is presented here.[1] This program can be used as a model in setting up other programs that would relate to helping a child learn to walk, crawl, grasp, and manipulate objects. The objective sought in this program was to help the parents structure the environment to encourage the child to assume sitting behavior. A description of the program follows.

A PROGRAM TO ENCOURAGE SITTING-UP BEHAVIOR

When a child is slow to develop the head, trunk, and extremity control necessary for sitting, various measures may be taken to strengthen such control, with consultation from a pediatrician and physical therapist. The suggested program is as follows:

1. Place the child in an upright sitting position for ten to thirty minutes three times a day. He could sit up in an infant seat or be propped up in the crib or on a sofa.

2. Pull the child up from a supine to sitting position fifteen times, three times daily. The mother should have the child hold onto her hands and then pull the child up. There may be considerable head lag at first; lessening of the degree of head lag is an indication of progress.

3. Place the child on a firm, safe surface such as the playpen or floor for at least thirty minutes a day. Crawling is encouraged by putting something of interest just outside the child's reach.

4. While the child is in a sitting position, tilt him from one side to the other, encouraging him to extend his arm and hand to catch himself on each side.

The record form shown on p. 91 is an example of how one might have the parents keep track of a daily pull-up program.

The parents should note on the record any days when the child was ill or particularly resistant to the exercise. If the nurse finds, in reviewing the record, that the parents have carried out the program consistently, she should mention the fact and encourage them to keep it up. If they have not carried out the program consistently, she should explore the reasons and then make suggestions which, if followed, may enable or encourage them to carry out the program. A retarded child's slow rate of progress can be discouraging to parents. The record forms and the nurse's acknowledgment are important additional incentives to some parents.

Name _____

Date _____

CIRCLE THE APPROXIMATE NUMBER OF PULL-UPS DONE

Week 1

	Monday	Tuesday	Wednesday	Thursday	Friday	Saturday	Sunday
Morning	5 10 15	5 10 15	5 10 15	5 10 15	5 10 15	5 10 15	5 10 15
Noon	5 10 15	5 10 15	5 10 15	5 10 15	5 10 15	5 10 15	5 10 15
Evening	5 10 15	5 10 15	5 10 15	5 10 15	5 10 15	5 10 15	5 10 15

Week 2

	Monday	Tuesday	Wednesday	Thursday	Friday	Saturday	Sunday
Morning	5 10 15	5 10 15	5 10 15	5 10 15	5 10 15	5 10 15	5 10 15
Noon	5 10 15	5 10 15	5 10 15	5 10 15	5 10 15	5 10 15	5 10 15
Evening	5 10 15	5 10 15	5 10 15	5 10 15	5 10 15	5 10 15	5 10 15

With most children there is some measureable progress within two months. The following "Tool for Assessment of Sitting-Up Ability" may be used prior to starting the sitting-up program and as a means of recording progress in head, trunk, and extremity control as the program is carried out. This is an example of breaking down a behavior to small but observable steps. In this program, the baby's development should progress in the order indicated under each of the four positions.

Name_____ Assessment number_____

Age _____ Date _____

TOOL FOR ASSESSMENT OF SITTING-UP ABILITY[1]

+ = present   o = not present   H = by history
± = fluctuating   n = not observed   na = not applicable

Pulling to sitting position

_____ 1. Complete head lag.
_____ 2. Partial head lag (lifts head up in last part of movement).
_____ 3. Slight head lag during first part of rising movement, but able to erect head before halfway to sitting position.
_____ 4. No head lag.
_____ 5. Flexion of extremities is noticeably tonic rather than deliberate.
_____ 6. Lower extremities flexed to give aid (pushing action) in the rising movement.

Sitting position

_____ 1. Head sags forward with chin resting on chest.
_____ 2. Head sags forward, but infant lifts it up for seconds at a time.
_____ 3. Head erect but bobbing.
_____ 4. Head held steady.
_____ 5. Shows some active balance—sits alone leaning forward, propping self with hands on legs.
_____ 6. Sits alone unsupported.
_____ 7. When the trunk is swayed by the examiner, the head always sways with it or plunges forward.
_____ 8. When the trunk is swayed, the head remains steady.
_____ 9. Back unevenly rounded.
_____10. Back has only a lumbar curvature.

Prone position

_____ 1. Infant can lift chin off surface momentarily.

_____ 2. Lifts chin off surface so that the plan of the face is at a 45-degree angle.

_____ 3. Lifts chin off surface so that head is at a 90-degree angle.

_____ 4. Holds chin and shoulders off surface, bearing weight on forearm. Holds head erect and rotates it.

_____ 5. Head is held well lifted with weight of body on the abdomen and hands.

_____ 6. Pivots body—moves in a circle in one spot by by crossing one arm over the other.

_____ 7. Crawling movement of extremities.

_____ 8. Legs extended.

_____ 9. Turns from prone to supine position.

Supine position

_____ 1. Tonic neck reflex (head turned far to side, one arm in extension to the side, the other arm flexed close to the shoulder or occiput).

_____ 2. Can elicit tonic neck reflex.

_____ 3. Head lifted as though striving to sit up. Legs lifted in extension.

_____ 4. Rolls part way to side.

_____ 5. Rolls from supine to prone.*

---

*Adapted from LeLouis, M.: An experimental program to increase sitting-up behavior in normal and deviant infants, Proceedings of the Fourth National Workshop for Nurses in Mental Retardation, University of Miami, April 4 to 7, 1967, sponsored by Children's Bureau, U. S. Department of Health, Education, and Welfare and Child Development Center.

REFERENCE

1. LeLouis, M.: An experimental program to increase sitting-up behavior in normal and deviant infants, Proceedings of the Fourth National Workshop for Nurses in Mental Retardation, University of Miami, April 4 to 7, 1967, sponsored by Children's Bureau, U. S. Department of Health, Education, and Welfare and Child Development Center.

ADDITIONAL READING

McGraw, M. B.: The neuromuscular maturation of the human infant, New York, 1943, Columbia University Press.

8
Self-feeding

DETERMINING READINESS

Self-feeding is the first major self-help skill developed by children. Readiness for this task is determined by the presence of a combination of neurological, physical, and physiological elements. In evaluating a child's readiness, the nurse needs to review all data about his development that might be pertinent. Using a multidisciplinary team evaluation, she might first appraise the information provided by the dentist, which may reveal such factors as lack of tooth eruption, atypical mouth, or tongue thrust. The physical examination by the pediatrician might reveal that the roof of the mouth is patent or confirm that seizures take place. The nutritionist may suggest a change in eating habits, an introduction to new foods, or a modification in consistency of food. If an inadequate diet is noted in the evaluation, it would be important to make sure that the child has an adequate nutritional intake before teaching the self-feeding task.

Next, appraise the child in regard to his stage of motor development. If the child's developmental level leaves him unprepared to accomplish self-feeding, the nurse must shift her attention to teaching the smaller skills that lead to self-feeding. To be ready to learn how to feed himself with a spoon, the child must be able to hold his head steady without support, sit up without losing balance, bring his hands to his mouth, and keep a grasp on a spoon. If head and neck control are not developed, the focus of intervention should be on promoting motor development. This would involve exercises that would also develop the child's ability to sit up. He may need passive and active hand exercises to promote grasping of a spoon. Plans for such therapy should be approved by the consulting physician and physical therapist.

Results of observations using an inventory such as the *Washington Guide,* as well as the data provided by others who have evaluated the child, will indicate the child's level of readiness. The presence or absence of skills used in self-feeding may be noted when the child is at play as well as at mealtime. For example, if he picks up a toy and puts it in his mouth, this serves as reliable evidence of the presence of hand-mouth coordination.

A composite of the age-appropriate suggested activities for enhancing the attainment of self-feeding skills is presented from the *Washington Guide.*

SUGGESTED ACTIVITIES IN RELATION TO AGE FOR ENHANCING FEEDING SKILLS

1 to 3 months
1. Consider change in nipple or positioning if infant has difficulty in swallowing.
2. Pace feeding tempo to infant's needs.
3. Hold him in comfortable, relaxed position while feeding.
4. Introduce solids, one kind at a time (use small spoon, place food well back on infant's tongue).

4 to 8 months
1. Give finger foods to develop chewing, stimulate gums, and encourage hand-to-mouth motion (cubes of cheese, bananas, dry toast, bread crust, cookies).
2. Encourage upright supported position for feeding.
3. Promote bottle holding.
4. Introduce junior foods.

9 to 12 months
1. Bring child in highchair to table and include for part of or for entire meal with family.
2. Have child dry and in comfortable position, with trunk and feet supported.
3. Encourage self-help in feeding.
4. Offer a spoon when interest is indicated.
5. Introduce cup or glass with small amount of fluid.
6. Begin use of table foods.

13 to 18 months
1. Continue offering finger foods (wieners, sandwiches).
2. Use nontip dishes and cups. Dishes should have sides to make filling of spoon easy.
3. Give opportunity for self-feeding.
4. Provide fluids between meals rather than having child fill up on fluids at mealtime.

19 to 30 months
1. Encourage self-feeding with spoon.
2. Do not rush child.
3. Serve foods plainly but attractively.
4. Small servings will encourage eating.

31 to 48 months
1. Encourage self-help.
2. Give opportunity for pouring (give rice in pitcher to promote pouring skills).
3. Encourage child to help set table.
4. Have well-defined rules about table manners.

49 to 52 months
1. Socialize with child at mealtime.
2. Have child help with preparation, table setting, and serving.
3. Include child in conversations at mealtimes by planning special times for him to tell about event, situations, or what he did during the day.

The following is a description of a feeding session written by a nurse before any intervention took place:

> Jim showed little interest in eating. He did not look at or touch the bowl or spoon, nor did he open his mouth in anticipation of food. Occasionally he gazed up at his mother, half-grinned, and laughed. She immediately smiled and laughed in response. Jim was very interested in his brother, who tried to stay within sight and who frequently talked to him and offered him toys. Mrs. M. tried at times to "shoo" the brother away; at other times she interrupted the feeding session to comply with one of his wishes.
>
> Jim did not sit well in the highchair. He gradually slipped down until he hung rather precariously. Mrs. M. then put her hand under his shoulder and hoisted him up. Jim frequently kicked his highchair, twisted his body, tossed his head, pounded on the chair, and ground his teeth.
>
> A bowl and spoon were placed before him on two occasions during this period. He showed no awareness of their presence, not even glancing at them. Observation during play revealed hand-mouth ability with toys.

In planning a systematic approach to teaching self-feeding skills, the nurse will find that recording the eating behavior of the child is indispensable. She should be alert for such behavior as his looking at his food, seeing his spoon, reaching for and grasping the spoon, the methods he uses to gain attention in the feeding process, and the hand movements he can make. How his particular responses affect his mother's reactions to him should be noted.

Certain essential information about the methods being used to enhance feeding should be obtained from the mother—how consistent she is in her approach, her use of imitative models, her expectations in performance, whether she is providing a quiet, nondistracting environment, her understanding of the fact that many small steps are involved in completing the task, whether she is feeding the child throughout the day and creating a factor of satiation, the appropriateness of foods she is serving to him, and his characteristic patterns of appetite.

Readiness of the mother to become involved in a teaching program is vital for success to occur. This may be determined by the verbal clues she gives, her expressed willingness to participate, the records she keeps, her ability to share observations, questions she asks, and her beginning attempts to carry through a planned program.

TECHNIQUES OF TEACHING

Adherence to a systematic approach is extremely important in producing desired changes in eating behavior. Accomplishment of self-feeding is probably one of the most highly structured learning experiences for a child. The nurse should become accustomed to the concept of breaking a task into its component parts and helping the child put these parts together. The following are the separate actions that a child goes through when feeding himself[1] :

1. Orients to food by looking at it
2. Looks at spoon
3. Reaches for spoon
4. Touches spoon
5. Grasps spoon
6. Lifts spoon
7. Delivers spoon to bowl
8. Lowers spoon into food
9. Scoops food onto spoon
10. Lifts spoon
11. Delivers spoon to mouth
12. Opens mouth
13. Inserts spoon into mouth
14. Moves tongue and mouth to receive food
15. Closes lips
16. Chews food
17. Swallows food

18. Returns spoon to bowl

The first three steps are the ones that should be built up before teaching the sequences that follow.

Include the mother in the observing and planning, emphasizing a systematic and consistent approach. This orientation will help her in teaching other self-help skills, as well as feeding. Plan to have her assume as much of the teaching responsibility as possible. This will help improve her feelings of adequacy as a mother. A letter one nurse[2] used to clarify the feeding program with the mother and the mother's outline of the child's self-feeding program illustrate one approach the nurse might use in helping the mother assume the teaching responsibility.

Dear Mrs. Smith,

I realize many of the things you and I have been doing the past few days are new. Therefore I've written for you some of the principles and procedures involved in using a behavioral approach to teach feeding skills. I hope this helps clarify some points; I know I had to continually refer to a book or an article when I first learned about these techniques.

I reviewed the base line data that I gathered during the first feeding observation April 19. From this we could see that Susie possessed the needed behaviors for self-feeding. She looked at the food, opened her mouth when you brought the spoon toward her, reached for and grasped objects and food, brought objects to her mouth, and chewed and swallowed. Then we decided to try *shaping* technique initially. *Shaping* is a process by which a successive approximation of behaviors is reinforced or rewarded. Basic behaviors are required first before reinforcement is given. For example, I tapped the spoon on the table. When Susie looked at it, I reinforced her behavior (looking at the spoon) by immediately giving her a bite of food. Gradually, more was required of her behaviors before she was reinforced with bites of food. For example, I did not give her a bite only for looking at the spoon but withheld a bite of food until she looked at the spoon and then moved her hand toward the spoon, then finally touched it, then picked it up.

After seeing how rapidly Susie learned to pick up the spoon, we began *fading* techniques. This is the technique you are presently using. You place your hand over Susie's and go through the activity of her lifting the spoon, dipping it into the bowl to get food, bringing the spoon to her mouth, and taking a bite. Gradually you "fade out" your participation in the activity. For example, as soon as you note that Susie can grasp the spoon independently, you may move your hand to her wrist during the feeding procedure or, as we have been doing, lighten your touch on Susie's hand during the feeding activities until she is just ready to take a bite. At this time, you can apply a little pressure in guiding the spoon to her mouth so that she doesn't twist and turn it. You may also remove your hand until she gets the spoon close to her mouth. Susie still has some difficulty in getting food on her spoon; however, she will refine this activity after practice. We can't expect perfection from a new behavior that requires practice.

In using this technique, you are applying two *positive reinforcers,* or rewards: (1) the natural reinforcer of food and (2) the reinforcer of your approval and attention. By *pairing* these two reinforcers (that is, at the same time Susie takes a bite or drink, you give her verbal praise, a hug, or smile at her) the acquired reinforcer of parental approval or attention helps strengthen Susie's feeding behaviors that preceded the reinforcement. Also, parental and social approval become very strong postive reinforcers (as we might see in our own lives and activities). By withdrawing or withholding positive reinforcement (that is, taking away food, not giving her your praise or attention), the behavior you do not desire is not strengthened; gradually these undesired behaviors will drop off or "extinguish."

Observation and data collection are also important steps, for several reasons. Remember the observations we made in the normal feeding situation—this was *base line data collection.* We will continue to record Susie's behaviors at mealtime so that after a period of time we can look at the data and actually see if the plan we're using has helped. If we cannot see an increase in desired behaviors, we must revise or adjust something. By collecting and recording data, we don't have to guess if our plan has worked but can actually see the results.

On the next page I have listed the techniques you are now using and indicated the goals we will aim for and the changes required. Mrs. Smith, you've done a beautiful job thus far. Remember the important, thing is consistency with this technique at every meal. Before long, you'll really be an expert.

Sincerely,

Mary North

SUSIE'S SELF-FEEDING PROGRAM

1. Prepare for the feeding situation. Have the necessary utensils and foods within reach.

2. Place the dish on the table with the spoon beside it.

3. a. Susie picks up the spoon.

b. She moves the spoon to the dish and gets food on it. (Try letting Susie do this independently, and remember that she will probably have some difficulty and take some "empty bites.")

c. Susie lifts the spoon toward her mouth. (During this behavior, you will probably have to place your hand on hers to help prevent her twisting and turning the spoon before the bite is taken. With practice Susie will develop skill in not spilling food from the spoon. You will be able gradually to fade out your participation in this behavior as Susie does better.)

4. Susie takes a bite. (Simultaneously, as the bite is taken, give Susie praise.)

5. If Susie shows inappropriate or unwanted behaviors (for example, looking around, spitting food, clapping her hands, playing with food, spoon, glass, or bowl, or throwing the spoon or glass), immediately remove food and spoon to the kitchen table and look away from her for about ten seconds. Then present the same food to her. If she repeats this undesired behavior cycle several times, either offer her another food or finish the meal. If another food is offered, wait approximately twenty seconds.

6. If Susie continues to want milk rather than food, offer milk in the glass after she has completed or eaten most of her meal. (Water may be given as desired between meals.)

7. Continue to keep the dietary records.

8. Record for each meal the approximate number of bites of food taken, drinks from the glass, and distracting behaviors. I will continue to come out and observe two or three mornings a week, if it's convenient for you.

In recording numbers of bites, etc., you might find it easy to mark with your free hand (if you've got one free!) on a piece of scrap paper. You could make three columns: one for bites of food, one for drinks from the glass by herself, and one for any type of distracting behaviors. I realize it will be impossible to get an exact record of these behaviors, but an inexact one is better than nothing.

9. Keep up the good work! You're doing a *fine job!*

Remember that the mother may have been working diligently with feeding for a long time without getting anywhere. To see her child feeding himself at last can create in the mother feelings of success, perhaps for the first time. Before beginning the teaching, however, explain that there will probably be extra spilling and messiness and that all children are messy when first learning to eat. Make provision for it by spreading papers, having extra cleaning rags available, and tying a bib on the child. Be prepared, too, to help in cleaning up.

Of critical importance for successful teaching is the reinforcement of desired responses. In teaching self-feeding you have the advantage of being able immediately to dispense a rather powerful reinforcer—food. The praise that is given at the same time is also effective.

As you and the mother work with the child, be alert at all times to securing and maintaining the attention of the child and minimizing distractions. In the beginning it may be necessary to have a radio, TV set, washer, and dryer turned off and to eliminate door slamming and the presence of other children vying for attention. Have toys out of the way and the table or highchair clear of unnecessary dishes and food.

Keep the child comfortable and secure. He should be warm and dry and in familiar surroundings with familiar persons present.

Correct posture encourages the child to use the motor skills he has developed and reduces the possibility of choking. He should be seated upright with back, trunk, and feet firmly supported.

The following preparatory steps are recommended:

1. Position the child on a chair. The child may need to be supported in the upright position with pillows or by placing a diaper around each thigh and tying it to the back of the chair. Tie on a bib that extends to the waist.

2. Have utensils and food (thick food that adheres to the spoon) within your reach on the table.

3. Place yourself in a comfortable position to the child's side. Your position should make it possible for you to observe arm movements, his line of vision, and his head motions. It should also be such that you can guide the child's feeding actions if necessary.

There are two main approaches that can be used in teaching spoon feeding. The first adopts the fading technique. With this method the nurse begins by firmly grasping the child's hand and guiding him through the feeding motions. As the child starts to carry out the motions himself, the nurse loosens her grasp and allows her guidance to "fade." This method should be used with a child who is limited in development or who has difficulty with motor coordination. The steps in this approach follow.

1. Get the child settled comfortably and securely at the table.

2. Determine your most comfortable working and teaching position.

3. Try to think of yourself as *this child.* ("I am his thoughts and hands for this feeding session.")

4. Introduce the spoon and get the child's attention on it by:

    a. Tapping it.

    b. Talking—"Look at the spoon."

    c. Turning the child's head in the direction of the spoon.

    d. Guiding the child's hand in touching it.

5. Give enthusiastic verbal praise every time the child makes an attempt to reach, touch, grasp, or move the spoon.

6. Do not allow the child to have the satisfaction of food unless he is holding the spoon (you may have to grasp his hand and guide him.) No finger feeding should be allowed.

7. Use active hand guidance to go through the feeding process. *Do not guide him passively through any of the feeding stages when he is not looking at the spoon or bowl, since he will not learn if he does not see what he is doing.*

Mother's hand guides the child's hands through the motions in learning self-feeding: a beginning step used with the technique of fading.

8. Move the spoon to the bowl, scoop the food, deliver the spoon to his mouth.

9. Gradually decrease your grasp of the child's hand over a period of time. Increase your expectations for improved performance but remember that repetition of the last step mastered is always the starting point for teaching the next step.

10. As you scoop food with your hand over his, exaggerate the scooping motion for emphasis.

11. Always be alert to changes in muscle tension in the child's hand as he exerts his own effort and begins to take over feeding himself.

12. The first independent effort will probably occur just before food enters his mouth. Loosen your grasp on his hand for this instant, but keep your hand positioned to exert full control as he moves the spoon from his mouth back toward the bowl.

The distance covered by independent effort will increase gradually until the child can bring food from bowl to mouth without your guidance.

13. Reward the child for effort throughout the procedure.

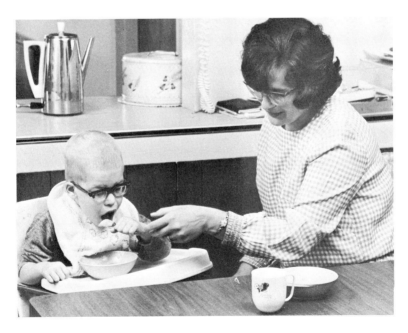

Mother decreases her guidance of actual hand movement: a phase of the fading process.

Expectations for independence are scaled to the child's performance. Getting food into the mouth is often the first successful independent achievement!

    a. Be sure to give almost constant verbal approval for successes. Pleasant tone of voice, cheerful mood, and other rewarding touches are important.

    b. Be sure he gets some food to his mouth regularly—by your active guidance if necessary.

14. To avoid behavior that will interrupt the feeding sequence of hand to spoon, spoon to bowl, food to mouth, you may have to guide him very firmly. Remember that nonfeeding behavior has become established and has to be dislodged.

    a. Try to ignore interrupting behavior by keeping him busy scooping with the spoon, getting it to his mouth and back to the bowl for another scoop.

    b. After the child understands and demonstrates that he can follow, for the most part, the motion of self-feeding, it may be helpful to remove food immediately from his reach when he behaves unacceptably. Return the food only when acceptable behavior resumes—when he is sitting quietly, ready to eat again.

The second approach to teaching self-feeding is referred to as a shaping approach. It, too, involves a systematic reinforcing of the steps toward a desired goal and ignoring of nonessential behavior. The major difference between fading and shaping is that physical assistance is not practiced in the latter method. Skills that the child has are "shaped" by reinforcement into a self-feeding pattern. The child thus generates more skilled and complex behavior patterns from present but incomplete responses.

The nurse might initially reward the child for attending to the spoon. When that response becomes automatic, a higher level of behavior should be expected before a reward is given. Subsequent responses to be learned would be reaching for, grasping, and holding the spoon. These responses would also be reinforced until they become established. Expectations and reinforcement for a higher level would be dependent on mastery of the previous step. When the child can hold the spoon, expectations would be placed on scooping and filling the spoon. The next steps are guiding the spoon to the mouth and inserting it. The giving of reinforcement by the nurse would end as the child becomes able to provide his own reinforcement.

Keep in mind that the child has the task of finding out what the adults' expectations are for his behavior. He cannot be expected to learn if he is confused about what they want. The mother should present cues that are distinct and consistent. If she has not allowed a particular form of behavior at one point, she should continue to make it clear that such behavior is not permissible. You want the child to learn to discriminate between what actions are going to produce positive reinforcement (food) and what will result in withdrawal or withholding of positive reinforcement. Keep in mind that you must repeatedly demonstrate to the child what is not allowed and what will be rewarded.

The following case illustration outlines the steps that were carried out in implementing a self-help feeding program for a 5½-year-old boy with Down's syndrome. A summary of the preliminary observations that were made to determine the child's readiness for feeding, as well as his mother's interactions during the feeding situation, is presented, along with the results of an assessment done with the *Washington Guide,* a history from the mother, and direct observations that were made on home visits. Also included is a prospective plan that the nurse implemented from the very beginning with the mother's help and the progressive success that was generated in using a consistent approach.

AN INDIVIDUALIZED APPROACH IN TEACHING A CHILD INDEPENDENCE IN SELF-FEEDING

Preliminary observations were made on a 5½-year-old male with Down's syndrome to determine his developmental level of functioning. According to the functional screening tool, gross motor abilities were at the level of 18 to 21 months of age, play skills at the level of 9 to 12 months of age and, his expressive language level was at the level of 36 weeks of age. There was a lack of development in all the self-help skills documented by observation.

A history from his mother indicated that he could hold a spoon but always dropped it into the bowl immediately. He could hold his own bottle but did not finger feed. A home visit made at lunchtime revealed that the child took his mother by the hand and led her to the kitchen sink, making whining noises as he did this. As she began to prepare lunch, he ran to the table and sat down to wait. He continued to whine until she set the food in front of him. He was sitting at a standard-sized table on an adult-sized chair. He was fed blended meats, vegetables, and salad in one large bowl with a large spoon. During feeding the child touched neither the dish nor the food while the mother sat in front of him. As he was being fed, he kept his hands on his lap and was very quiet and motionless except for opening his mouth at fast-paced intervals. As the spoon was delivered to his mouth, he fixed his vision on both the food and the spoon. When the dish was empty, he looked at it and started whining. He then got off his chair and took his mother by the hand, pulling her toward the sink, gesturing and pointing to more food. In response to this, the mother prepared a large bowl of applesauce, and the routine was repeated. The mother was requested to hand the spoon to the child. The child grasped and held it briefly and dropped it into the bowl. He then reached for his mother's hand and guided it to the spoon handle. After she fed him by spoon again, the child climbed down from the chair, grabbed some plastic blocks, and began to mouth them.

Clearly the child had the essential motor behaviors that could be programed into self-feeding behaviors. He exhibited the ability of hand-to-mouth coordination, could support himself alone in a chair, closed his mouth while swallowing, and could, in fact, connect a spoon-to-bowl-to-mouth relationship. This information alone was enough for a decision to implement some programed instruction for the mother. The public health nurse doing the follow-up study of the family was familiar with the principles of behavior modification. The main principles she planned to follow in executing a program for self-feeding included the following:

1. Concentration on the use of positive reinforcement following desirable behavior.

2. Delivering reinforcement promptly following the desired behavior.

3. Using continuous reinforcement while establishing certain behaviors and then using intermittent reinforcement to maintain the desired response.

4. Rewarding small increments and building up simple behaviors toward a more complicated chain of responses.

5. Ignoring undesirable behavior and removing food when inappropriate behaviors were demonstrated.

6. Programing was to consist of systematically dispensing positive and negative reinforcement contingent on behavior emitted and requiring more skilled behavior as each sequence was met with successful mastery.

The public health nurse explained to the mother that she would initiate a self-feeding program immediately with the mother's cooperation. She was careful in her explanation that the child was to be taught with a systematic and consistent approach. She avoided such terms as "rewards" and "punishment" that would be given or withheld.

The mother enthusiastically prepared the child for the teaching experience by initially preparing for spilling of food, a natural phenomenon accompanying self-feeding for the first time.

It was resolved early that the public health nurse would commence the feeding plan only if the child had not been fed since breakfast, thus establishing food as a more powerful and durable primary reinforcer.

At the beginning of the session the public health nurse was careful to posture the child in a comfortable sitting-up position and seated close to her, so that she made provisions for a carefully structured environment. She initially gained the child's attention by tapping the spoon next to the bowl full of food. The child looked at both the food and the spoon and turned his head to look at the public health nurse. Since no food was forthcoming, he grabbed for the bowl of food, which was immediately removed. A pattern of reinforcement begins primarily in this interaction. The child is losing a primary reinforcer. The undesirable behavior of grabbing for the bowl is not being reinforced or strengthened. The bowl was again placed next to the spoon and the behavior was repeated. Again the nurse quickly withdrew the positive reinforcer (food). When the bowl was replaced the third time, the nurse again tapped the spoon to secure the child's attention to it. The child's response was to turn his head and grab for her arm, placing it next to the food. This behavior was ignored. The child then reached for the spoon and was immediately lavished with flowering praise. "Good boy, Robert!" The child then dropped the spoon, and the bowl was withdrawn— again, the removal of a positive reinforcer. One sees a consistent pattern of reinforcement emerging here with the systematic subtraction of the food, a known positive reinforcer. Again the child reached for the spoon, this time holding it longer and directing it to the bowl. Praise was given for this and guidance of the spoon into the bowl and assistance in delivering the spoon with food to his mouth. Each successive time, the child was required to reach for the spoon and direct it to the bowl. These movements were immediately reinforced by subsequent assistance to get food into his mouth. Attempts at getting food onto the spoon were reinforced by assistance, thus the prediction of a forthcoming positive reinforcer. The next step was to withhold assistance while requiring scooping movements. Many trial-and-error movements of scooping food were established until the child was coordinated enough to get food on the spoon alone. The adult's participation was rapidly withdrawn, since the child was in greater control and successful in feeding.

The child's mother had observed the techniques closely and was anxious to participate. The mother was observed to follow through the same routine in a systematic and orderly fashion. The mother exhibited immediate finesse with instruction, quickly becoming discriminated as one who either dispensed positive reinforcement or withheld it, contingent on the child's behavior.

REFERENCES

1. Powell, M.: An interpretation of effective management and discipline of the mentally retarded child, Nursing Clinics of North America, Philadelphia, 1966, W. B. Saunders Co.
2. Colleran, N.: Case study (unpublished).

ADDITIONAL READINGS

Barnard, K.: Teaching the retarded child is a family affair, Amer. J. Nurs. **68**:305-311, 1968.
Bensberg, G. J.: Teaching the mentally retarded: a handbook for ward personnel, Atlanta, 1965, Southern Regional Education Board.
Bensberg, G. J., Colwell, C. N., and Cassel, R. H.: Teaching the profoundly retarded self-help activities by behavior shaping techniques, Amer. J. Ment. Defic. **69**:674-679, 1965.
Karen, R. L., and Maxwell, S. J.: Strengthening self-help behavior in the retardate, Amer. J. Ment. Defic. **71**:546-550, 1967.
Whitney, L.: Operant learning theory: a framework deserving nursing investigation, Nurs. Res. **15**:229-235, Summer, 1966.
Whitney, L., and Barnard, K.: Implication of operant learning theory for nursing care of the retarded child, Men. Retard. **3**:26-29, 1966.
Zieler, M. D., and Jervey, S. S.: Development of behavior: self-feeding, J. Consult. Psychol. **32**:164-168, 1969.

9
Toileting

It is advisable that a child first master the skills in self-feeding before his toilet training is started, since this is the normal sequence of development. The activities from the *Washington Guide* that are specific to encouraging independent toileting behavior are listed.

SUGGESTED ACTIVITIES IN RELATION TO AGE TO ENCOURAGE INDEPENDENT TOILETING

9 to 12 months
1. Watch for clues that indicate that child is wet or soiled.
2. Be sure to change diapers when wet or soiled so that child begins to experience contrast between wetness and dryness.

13 to 18 months
1. Sit child on toilet or potty chair at regular intervals for short periods of time throughout day.
2. Praise child for success.
3. If potty chair is used, it should be located in bathroom.
4. Respond promptly to signals and clues of child by taking him to bathroom or changing his pants.
5. Use training pants once toilet training is begun.

19 to 30 months
1. Continue regular intervals of toileting.
2. Reward success.

3. Dress child in simple clothing that he can manage.
4. Remind him occasionally, particularly after mealtime, juice time, naptime, and playtime.
5. Take him to bathroom before bedtime.
6. Bathroom should be convenient to use, the door easy to open.
7. Plan to begin training when disruptions in regular routine are at a minimum, e.g., don't begin during vacation trip.

31 to 48 months
1. Child may still need reminding.
2. Dress him in simple clothing that he can manage.
3. Ignore accidents; refrain from shame or ridicule.

49 to 52 months
1. Praise child for his accomplishment.

READINESS

In preparing to help a mother toilet-train her retarded child, refer again to the total evaluation of the child. Information sources are the multidisciplinary team work-up, the interview on the mother's child-rearing practices, and the *Washington Guide.* By referring to the guide, the nurse can ascertain what level the child has attained in motor development. Children are considered physically ready for training if they can stand and walk alone. The ability to walk indicates that the spinal tracts are myelinated to the level of the bowel and bladder sphincters and that the child is physiologically capable of sphincter control.

When a child can be considered physically ready for training, ask the mother to begin keeping a daily record of the times at which elimination occurs, the times at which liquids are taken, and the amounts of liquid taken. The mother's immediate response when elimination occurs should also be recorded. One mother may immediately change the diaper as soon as she notices it is wet; another may often wait ten to thirty minutes until she has finished doing something. The mother's pattern of response is an important consideration in devising the teaching plan.

The mother should be provided with a chart form such as the one shown here for recording the information. Emphasize to her the usefulness of the information in planning. A mother's cooperation in keeping the record is often an indication of her commitment to follow through with training.

Keep a record that includes the following:
    Time of wetting and soiling
    Child's response and mother's response
    Intake of fluids

Time wet or soiled	Child's response	Mother's response	Intake
9:30 Soiled	Irritable	Changed pants right away	

1. Recording should be done for three or four days or until a pattern is set (when you note that the child is wet about every two hours and bowel movements are generally at the same time of day).

2. Keep the record form in a convenient place, perhaps taped to the bathroom door.

3. If urination is more frequent than once an hour, check with the family physician to see if there is a physical problem.

4. If the child is ill or fluid intake patterns change temporarily, it is not advisable to collect base line information.

These records serve as guides. The child is ready to start training when he:

1. Can retain urine for about two hours and is having one or two bowel movements a day

2. Can walk (unless there is a physical handicap preventing walking)

3. Shows some sign of awareness of elimination such as changing facial expression, quietness, pulling at clothes, making different sounds, engaging in attention-getting activity, squirming, crossing legs, and irritability

4. Is able to feed himself

5. Is not sick

Before training is begun, environmental observations should be completed. A verbal report by the mother is not enough. A visit, or several visits, should be made to pick up information such as whether the child is being dressed in clothes that will not hinder training, whether the child is physically capable of climbing onto a toilet, whether the mother stays with the child in the bathroom during the initial attempts to regularize his schedule, and what the mother does if the child successfully eliminates when taken to the toilet. The child may still be in diapers. Since diapers are meant to be wet on, they are not appropriate for toilet training. The mother may be relying too much on talk in her attempts at training and not providing a highly structured situation to facilitate the child's mastery of the task. Sometimes mothers inadvertently create a punitive atmosphere because they do not concentrate on the child's need for praise.

The following points should be kept in mind:

1. Clothes should be easy to manage. Training pants with elastic waistbands should be used.

2. The bathroom should be convenient to use, with an easy-to-open door; it should be available most of the time.

3. The toilet should be easy for the child to use. He may need a footstool.

4. If a potty chair is used, it should be located in the bathroom.

5. The toilet should not be introduced to the child as a plaything.

6. Flushing of the toilet may frighten the child; when he is first learning to use the toilet, do not flush immediately after he uses it.

7. Toilet training should be started at a time when social disruptions are at a minimum (not when company is coming for a week).

8. The child should be taken to the bathroom at regular times. If he goes about every two hours, the schedule might be on arising, after meals, midmorning, midafternoon, and before bed. Consistency in following a schedule is very important.

9. Arrange the schedule so that the child is taken when family disruptions are at a minimum.

10. Interrupt training if the child becomes sick and requires an increased fluid intake.

TECHNIQUES OF TEACHING

Some appropriate reinforcers for producing and sustaining the desired behavior should be decided on with the mother in advance. What is most significant is the mother's recognition that a desired response should be followed by some special attention from her. It can be pointed out to her that most children constantly seek their mothers' attention. Attention can be a pat, a kiss, or words of approval. To be effective in training, attention must be given immediately after the desired behavior occurs. Such information may also encourage mothers of mentally retarded children to get into the habit of interacting positively with their children.

For some children the mother's praise or kiss is just as effective a reinforcer as concrete symbols such as a toy or piece of candy. Others respond much more readily, as far as training is concerned, to the concrete symbols. Of course, mothers should continue to give such children love and encouragement along with the concrete symbols. Once the training pattern is formed, praise and affection alone will probably be sufficient to sustain it.

Thus the mother should be advised to do the following in regard to reinforcement:

1. Determine what reinforcers would be appropriate—a smile, relaxed praise, food (raisin, cracker, etc.), touch.

2. Reinforce desired behavior immediately—right after the child eliminates on the toilet, helps to pull his pants down, indicates he has to go to the toilet, etc.

3. Do not scold, punish, or change expression when the child does not eliminate on the toilet, when he starts to play and does not attend to the training, when he wets his pants in between times, when he sits and screams.

Review with the mother the information she has been collecting on the child's habits of elimination. When together you have identified the times that the child is most likely to eliminate, point out to her that these are the specific times at which she should take the child into the bathroom. Emphasize to her that these are the most likely times for success in teaching. Usually these times will be fairly predictable—after a meal, juice time, exercise, or a long nap. Inform the mother that training efforts should be curtailed when the child is ill and fluid intake is increased. The mother should also be reminded to continue to be alert for changes in the child's behavior or appearance that are signs that he is about to eliminate.

At the specified times, the mother will lead the child into the bathroom and help him sit on the toilet, acknowledging and praising each step. She will then keep his attention on the task and respond when success is noted or remove the child if five or ten minutes have passed without any signs of elimination. The importance of staying with the child in the beginning stages of training should be made very clear to the mother. Training will progress if she is there to give some immediate form of recognition when the child does use the toilet. He will then be motivated to go to the bathroom again in order to receive his "reward."

The suggested teaching routine should include the following stages:

A. Anticipating needs
   1. Observe the child for indications of needing to eliminate and keep on regular schedule.
   2. Lead the child to the bathroom.
   3. The mother should do the following.

      a. Pull his pants down.

      b. Place the child on the toilet.

      c. If the child eliminates, reinforce with praise or food.

      d. Remove him from the toilet and pull up his pants.

      e. Wash and dry his hands.

B. When the mother observes the child indicating his needs to eliminate, then

    1. Have the child begin indicating his needs; he may still have to be taken on a regular schedule.

    2. The mother should have the child help pull his pants down by placing her hands on his and guiding.

    3. Help the child get onto the toilet.

    4. If elimination occurs, help the child with toilet tissue, guiding his hand.

    5. Help the child pull up his pants and wash and dry his hands.

    6. Give praise for each step he learns to complete independently.

C. Expect eventual independence; the mother may have to stand by while the child goes through the steps

    1. Goes to the bathroom by himself.

    2. Pulls his pants down.

    3. Gets on the toilet.

    4. Eliminates.

    5. Uses tissue.

    6. Gets off the toilet.

    7. Pulls his pants up.

    8. Flushes the toilet.

    9. Washes and dries his hands.

   10. Leaves the bathroom.

If the child fails on the first few trials of toileting, the mother should refrain from responding negatively. She should simply continue to take him to the bathroom at those times when he would most likely need to eliminate. During toilet training, mothers should give special attention to keeping their children dry and clean between eliminations. If they are kept dry, wetness becomes something that is unpleasant and to be avoided. When the child does begin to give cues of needing to go to the bathroom, the mother should take him there immediately, even if he happens to be involved in playing or another activity.

After the mother is well into the training process, review with her the matter of rewarding behavior that she wants to have repeated and overlooking behavior that she does not want repeated. Stress the essential point that the first small steps need to be reinforced immediately. If she is not making progress in training her child, she should ask herself: Am I applying rewards immediately? Have I been consistent in doing so? Am I carrying out the training step by step, according to the child's ability to learn, and not expecting too much too soon?

The chances are that the mother will see enough change in the child's performance to motivate her to continue with her efforts. Just the same, routinely acknowledge the efforts she is making too.

Children can learn by imitating others. Models for toileting may be provided by siblings or by arrangement at the nursery school.

In summary, these are the main points to keep in mind when helping mothers with the toilet training of their retarded children:

1. Ascertain motivation of the mother.
2. Record pertinent information.
3. Structure the environment for learning.
4. Dress the child in appropriate clothing.
5. Break the task down into small steps.
6. Ascertain the child's readiness (motor and physical).
7. Use appropriate rewards.
8. Acknowledge mastery of each small step.
9. Repeat trials.
10. Be consistent in procedure and in rewarding.
11. Provide models for imitation.

READINGS

Bensberg, G. J.: Teaching the mentally retarded: a handbook for ward personnel, Atlanta, 1965, Southern Regional Education Board.

Ellis, N. R.: Toilet training the severely defective patient: an S-R reinforcement analysis, Amer. J. Ment. Defic. **68:**98-103, 1963.

Hundziak, M., Maurer, R. A., and Watson, L. S., Jr.: Operant conditioning in toilet training of severely mentally retarded boys, Amer. J. Ment. Defic. **70:**120-124, 1965.

Kimbrell, D. L., Luckey, R. E., Barbuto, P., and Love, J. G.: Operation dry pants: an intensive habit-training program for severely and profoundly retarded, Ment. Retard. **5:**32-36, 1967.

Lohmann, W., Eyman, R. K., and Lask, E.: Toilet training, Amer. J. Ment. Defic. **71:**551-557, 1967.

Muellner, R. S.: Development of urinary control in children: some of the causes and treatment of primary enuresis, J.A.M.A. **172:**1256, 1960.

10
Dressing skills

Undressing and dressing consist of many small, discrete tasks. Fine discrimination and coordination are involved in such tasks as tying, buttoning, snapping, placing shoes on the correct feet, and getting garments on right side out and in the correct order. Thus, before effective skills in dressing can be mastered, the child must have attained a level of motor development that permits arm and leg extension, balance, finger dexterity, turning the hands palms up and down, a pincer grasp, and other motor skills.

READINESS

By reviewing evaluations of the child's motor development, by interviewing the mother, and by observing the child's behavior while he is being dressed or undressed, the overall level of the child's dressing abilities can be assessed. Good indications of his abilities may be observed also in his play activity. For example, the nurse may see the child stringing beads; this could be an indication that he has the coordination necessary for learning to lace shoes. Initial observations also include noting whether the mother has the child dressed in clothes that are easy to manage rather than in tight-fitting garments or in garments with small buttons, complicated criss-cross straps, or fasteners located high in the back.

A composite of general suggestions for parents to encourage the proper teaching of self-care activity in regard to dressing is included here. These are arranged in age-appropriate sequence.

SUGGESTED PRACTICES FOR ENCOURAGING THE ATTAINMENT OF DRESSING SKILLS BY THE CHILD

13 to 18 months
1. Encourage child to remove socks, etc. after task is initiated for him.
2. Do not rush child.
3. Have him practice with large buttons and with zippers.

19 to 30 months
1. Have child practice with large buttons.
2. Encourage and allow opportunity for self-help in many ways, including removing clothes, handwashing, getting a drink, etc.
3. Dress child in simple clothing.
4. Provide mirror at height at which child can observe himself for brushing his teeth, etc.

31 to 48 months
1. Provide him with his own dresser drawer.

2. Simple garments encourage self-help. Do not rush child.
3. Provide large buttons, zippers, slip-over clothing.
4. Self-handwashing, help with brushing teeth.
5. Provide regular routine for dressing in either bathroom or bedroom.
6. Mark garments to help identify front or back, e.g., at neckband of collar.

49 to 52 months
1. Assign regular task of placing clothes in hamper or basket.
2. Continue with simple clothing.
3. Encourage self-help in dressing and undressing.
4. Allow child to select clothes he will wear.

The mother's commitment and ability to follow through on teaching the child the tasks of dressing and undressing should be considered. Ask her how she intends to fit teaching into her daily routine: "Now, Mrs. X, how will you be able to take twenty minutes or so from your housework two or three times every day to teach Jimmy how to dress himself?" If the mother seems uncertain, go over her daily schedule with her and suggest changes. The teaching should be carried out on a regular basis. If she seems resistive to making time for teaching, it may be because she is doubtful about getting results. She should be assured that the chances of success are high and will increase as a proper teaching program is consistently carried out. Your demonstration of teaching may have the effect of convincing her that her child can learn more than she had thought.

TECHNIQUES OF TEACHING

As with other tasks, breaking the task of dressing down into its small component steps is important. Equally important is the immediate recognition given to the child when small steps are accomplished. The development of simple manipulative and perceptual responses is an important step toward dressing skills. Examples of such responses are looking at the part of the garment that is going to be pulled up or down, reaching for that section of clothing, and grasping and manipulating it.

The mother should teach the child how to undress before attempting to teach him how to dress. Undressing is easier because it does not involve handling the garments in a special order, getting them right side out, etc.

In teaching the child how to take off a shirt, begin by slipping it off almost completely and letting the child give it the last tug over the head. If necessary, place your hand over his to give a cue as to what you expect. Next time make the task a little more difficult by having him pull off the shirt from the neck instead of the head, then from the shoulders, then the chest, and finally the waist. Each time be sure you have the child's attention so that the teaching will not be lost.

Similarly, when teaching the child to put his arm in a sleeve, place the sleeve halfway up the arm and have the child complete pulling it all the way up. For trousers, pull them almost all the way up and let him complete the task. Next time leave the trousers slightly lower than before and again let the child pull them up. Continue until the child is pulling up the trousers from the ankles. At each step he performs successfully, praise abundantly. Again, do not expect much learning unless the child's attention is on what is being taught. You may want to direct his attention by gently placing your hands on either side of his face and turning his head toward what it is you want him to see.

Some children learn how to put on their coats by the following method:

1. The coat is placed on the back of the chair, just as if someone sitting in the chair had carefully slipped out of the coat and left it.
2. The child is seated in the chair.
3. The child is required to look at the right armhole.
4. His arm is placed in the armhole.
5. The child is required to look at the left armhole.
6. His left arm is placed in the armhole.
7. The coat is pulled on with a forward movement of both arms.

The mentally retarded child learns best by demonstration and redemonstration; verbal instruction alone cannot be relied on. The more complex the skill, however, the poorer the degree of imitation. This explains the necessity of breaking a task down into the component steps. Establishing routines for dressing also makes the tasks easier; for example, always dressing in the same place at the same time (a place where distractions are minimized) and keeping the clothes in the same place consistently.

The child should be dressed in simple, loose garments during his beginning attempts. When teaching the child to button and unbutton, have him practice first with large buttons.

Some simple "visual aids" that are often suggested to make dressing easier for the retarded child include marking one shoe with a colored dot on the outside of the heel, marking the back of clothing with a laundry marker, and sewing strips on the fronts of shirts and pants so that by lining up the strips he can get his clothes on straight. As the nurse works with any child, she will naturally discover techniques that are helpful to him, such as fastening a ring on the zipper pull. Creating a play situation often aids in learning. "Dress-up time" and lacing large shoes are two forms of play. The child may gladly dress and undress life-sized dolls and, in doing so, gain skill in dressing himself.

READINGS

Bensberg, G. J.: Teaching the mentally retarded: a handbook for ward personnel, Atlanta, 1965, Southern Regional Education Board.

Richert, G., Sloane, N., Sosnowski, G., and Weincrot, B.: Dressing techniques for the cerebral palsied child, Amer. J. Occup. Ther. 8:1, 1954.

11
Play

THE IMPORTANCE OF PLAY

Most children master their developmental tasks through play. There is a predictable sequential nature to the development of play, as there is in language and physical growth. Children progress from simple stages to complex levels in play as in other aspects of their growth and development.

The infant's initial experiences with play are of a simple nature. An infant can first be observed to play with his hands and feet. Much exploring of the early infant environment occurs as the infant sucks and touches objects with his mouth and tongue. There is a tendency to repeat activities that are gratifying. This play behavior can be seen as he babbles and coos and repeats noises of interest to him. He receives additive feedback if the sounds he makes are repeated for him.

A gradual complexity of play behaviors is seen as the environment is more actively and broadly explored and activities are coordinated. Problem solving, a longer attention span for certain tasks, more purposeful activities, and increasing social interactions with others take place as the child advances in play. For example, the child begins to explore and attend to the greater variety of objects available to him. He may consider an electric light socket a toy the first time; the second time, he won't regard it as such. In his world of small toys there are new surprises such as toys breaking, proving to belong to someone else, or being subject to confiscation by the child's superiors. Toys begin to provide children with a sense of possession. This involves having a toy for oneself and not hearing mother say "Leave that alone!"; it belongs to the child.

Through play the child learns to solve problems and his attention span grows. For instance, a small child first starts glancing at the television set, then he looks at commercials, then he gradually watches small cartoons, then he sees a short film to completion, and finally he is able to attend longer to a full film. Children's curiosity develops and their fantasy life widens and becomes more elaborate because of their exposure to play.

Significant advances are seen when a child spontaneously re-creates an activity after it has been successfully mastered through practicing imitation of others.

Varying and more complex social, motor, intellectual, and emotional involvements are expected as a child expands in his play experiences. Through play, children learn to share, to take their turns, to lose, and to cooperate. In games, children win and lose. Both goal achievement and accomplishment are involved in activities of play. A child's intellectual development is also affected by toys, games, and play interactions with others. Children engage in role playing. For example, in assuming the learner's role, you see children playing the learner in school before they ever enter the classroom.

Games, toys, and tools should be geared to the child's particular stage and pattern of maturation. As the child enlarges his acquaintance with his environment, balls, push-and-pull toys, and other objects become fascinating. Keep in mind that the child may show little interest in a toy until he becomes used to holding it and seeing it. Again the importance of maintaining the child's attention should be kept in mind. It may be possible to hold his attention, meaning eye contact, for only thirty seconds before he is distracted. This should be anticipated, and definite efforts to increase attention span should be made. Thus the parent could systematically give his attention when the child looks at or handles the toy and remove his attention when the child is not attending.

Toys are considered manageable for infants and children at different ages based on the criterion of how well they promote the auditory, visual, and kinesthetic senses and enhance gross and fine motor coordination. Since the infant first follows objects with his eyes, an object of a solid primary color that can be hung in easy view is suitable. Because motor control proceeds from the head and neck down to the shoulders, from the arms to the fingers, trunk, legs, and feet, it is advisable that toys for infants be selected on the basis that they will help promote the facilities for sight, for hearing, and for muscular activities of reaching, grasping, pushing, pulling, and movement of the arms and legs. When the child is about 1 to 2 years of age and is ambulating, he enjoys toys that help refine his gross motor movements. He is responsive to toys that require pushing and pulling to make them move and he enjoys toys that produce interesting noises. For 2- to 5-year-old children, it is recommended that toys be selected on the basis that the child is active, thus toys should provide the opportunity for him to exercise his large muscles and to refine even more precisely his gross motor skills.

The young child responds best to simple toys. From manipulating them, he learns to take things out of a container, to put them in, to place one thing on top of another, and to drop and eventually throw things. Playing with toys that require eye-hand coordination, such as hammers, blocks, and stacking rings, will help the child develop important motor skills, including those he needs for other, more functional skills such as self-feeding.

Imitative behavior can often be encouraged by letting the child play with the parent's old clothes and tools that are not a hazard to his safety. The child should also be encouraged to imitate siblings' behavior when that seems desirable.

In examining the developmental skills possible from the simple act of play with a ball, one realizes how necessary play is in the developmental course of a child.

DEVELOPMENT SKILLS THAT CAN BE LEARNED THROUGH BALL PLAY

1. Ball playing gives the child practice in neuromuscular coordination.
2. A child gets an exercise in problem solving.
3. He strengthens his spatial judgment perceptions.
4. He learns something about geometrical shapes.
5. A child learns that weights are involved and that textures are different.
6. A child can learn to take his turn and thus learn that there is sequence and order to a game.
7. Ball playing generally involves another person, so that the child learns a social give-and-take.
8. The child learns rules about where a ball can be played with.
9. There is positive ego involvement in skillfully catching a ball.
10. He learns to associate the word "ball" with an object that is round and thrown.

TECHNIQUES OF TEACHING AND ENRICHMENT

Parents should be encouraged to spend time helping their children develop exploratory play behavior. At first, this consists of the child's watching and reaching toward stimulating objects or people, then grasping toys and responding to sensory stimuli. This develops into the child's exploration of his own body. Games such as peek-a-boo and patty-cake provide both language and rhythm stimulation, as well as use of motor skills. Simple games of touch my nose, your nose, my mouth, your mouth, etc. are a form of pleasurable interchange between parents and child and over a period of time help the child establish a concept of his body and its functions. Generally children are fascinated by a mirror and can spend considerable time looking at themselves in it.

Colorful mobiles are especially good for the child whose environmental scope is limited because he is inactive or because he is confined to a small area. Such children are in special need of environmental stimuli. The level of perceptiveness of a child restricted to a crib many hours a day may be reduced. He sees so little going on about him that he does not develop the normal inclination to look around and explore.

Play behavior does not emerge automatically or by chance in the retarded child. The nurse should encourage the parents to play with the child for a set amount of time every day. Many parents have found it helpful to set aside a room or a corner where the child's playthings can be kept and which the child comes to know as the place for doing things with his parents and enjoying themselves.

The composites of suggested activities for both play behavior and language enrichment and stimulation are included in this chapter. It is believed that both of these areas represent a significant part of the child's learning and that parents should incorporate such suggestions to further the child's social and language development. Language enrichment can easily become a part of the child's play.

SUGGESTED ACTIVITIES FOR ENCOURAGING AGE-APPROPRIATE PLAY BEHAVIOR

1 to 3 months
1. Hold and touch child often.
2. Provide him with cradle gyms, mobiles, and brightly colored, visually interesting objects within arm's distance.
3. During waking hours, place child in room with people so that they can respond to him.

4 to 8 months
1. Begin patty-cake and peek-a-boo games.
2. Provide for periods of solitary play (playpen).
3. Hold and touch child often.
4. Provide variety of multicolored and multitextured objects, none smaller than 1 cubic inch, which child can hold.
5. Encourage exploration of body parts.
6. Provide floating toys for bath.

9 to 12 months
1. Continue mother-infant games.
2. Give child opportunity to place objects in containers and pour them out.
3. Provide him with large and small objects with which to play.
4. Encourage interactive play.

13 to 18 months
1. Introduce child to other children even though he may not play with them.
2. Provide music, books, and magazines.
3. Encourage imitative activities—helping with dusting, sweeping, and stirring.
4. Provide objects or toys that can be thrown without damage (balls, stuffed or inflated objects).
5. Remove from reach objects considered valuable by the family.

19 to 30 months
1. Provide with new materials for manipulating and feeling—finger paints, clay, sand, stones, water, and soap; wooden toys, cars, and animals; building blocks of various sizes; crayons and paper; rhythmical tunes and equipment such as swing, rocking chair, or rocking horse; children's books containing short, simple stories with repetition and familiar objects and brightly colored, simple pictures. Guide child's hand to participate actively in specific activities, e.g., using crayons and hammering.

31 to 48 months
1. Provide for play with small groups of children.
2. Encourage imaginative and dramatic play activities.
3. Encourage musical activities – singing, experimenting with musical instruments.
4. Encourage group participation in rhymes and dancing by hopping or jumping.
5. Encourage drawing and painting (seldom recognizable).

49 to 52 months
1. Provide with materials for painting and drawing. (Object will be out of proportion; details that are most important to child are drawn largest.)
2. Encourage printing of numbers and letters.
3. Provide with materials for working with clay (making recognizable objects) and cutting and pasting.
4. Provide with materials for building sturdy structures with boxes, chairs, barrels, etc.

SUGGESTED ACTIVITIES FOR ENCOURAGING LANGUAGE DEVELOPMENT

1 to 3 months
1. Observe facial expressions, gestures, postures, and movements when vocalizations are being produced.
2. Smile and talk softly in pleasant tone while holding, touching, and handling infant.
3. Interact frequently with infant for pleasure.
4. Refrain from letting infant cry (for over five minutes) without checking for possible causes.

4 to 8 months
1. Engage in smiling eye-to-eye contact while talking to infant.
2. Vocalize in response to inflectional patterns and when infant is producing babbling sounds. Repeat sounds he makes.
3. Vocalize with infant during feeding, bathing, dressing, diapering, bedtime preparation, and holding.
4. Stimulate laughing by light tickling.
5. Provide variety of sounds: bells, whistles, horns, phones, laughing, singing, talking, music box, noise-making toys, and common household noises.
6. While talking to infant, hold him so that he can see your face.
7. If crying or laughing sounds are not discerned at this stage, report to family physician, pediatrician, public health nurse, or well-child clinic.

9 to 12 months
1. Gain child's attention when giving simple commands.
2. Accompany oral directions with gestures.
3. Vocalize with child during feeding, bathing, and play.
4. Provide sounds that child can reproduce such as lip smacking and tongue clicking.
5. Repeat directions frequently and have child participate in actions such as opening and closing drawers and moving his arms and legs up and down.
6. Have child respond to verbal directions: "stand up," "sit down," "close the door," "open the door," "turn around," or "come here."

13 to 18 months
1. Incorporate repetition into daily routine of home. Feeding: name baby's food, his eating utensils, ask if he is enjoying his dessert. Concentrate on reviewing day's events in simple manner. Household duties: mother names each item as she dusts; names foods and utensils while cooking. Playing: identify toys when using them; explain their function.
2. Let child see mouthing of words.
3. Encourage verbalization and expression of wants.

19 to 30 months
1. Continue to present concrete objects with words. Talk about activities with which child is involved.
2. Include child in conversations during mealtimes.
3. Encourage speech by allowing child to express wants and giving him time to do so.
4. Incorporate games into bathing routine by having child name and point to body parts.
5. As child gains confidence in remembering and using words appropriately, encourage less use of gesture.
6. Count and name articles of clothing as they are placed on child.
7. Count and name silverware as it is placed on table.
8. Sort, match, and name glassware, laundry, cans, vegetables, and fruit with child.

31 to 36 months
1. Read stories with familiar content but

with more detail—nonsense rhymes, humorous stories.

2. Expect child to follow simple commands.
3. Give child opportunity to hear and repeat his full name.
4. Listen to child's explanation about pictures he draws.
5. Encourage child to repeat nursery rhymes by himself and with others.
6. Address child with his first name.

37 to 48 months

1. Use picture books.
2. Have child repeat story.
3. Arrange trips to zoo, farms, seashore, stores, and movies and discuss them with child.

4. Give simple explanations to questions.

49 to 52 months

1. Play games in which child names colors.
2. Encourage use of "please" and "thank you."
3. Encourage social verbal interactions with other children.
4. Encourage correct use of words.
5. Provide puppets or toys with movable parts that child can converse about.
6. Allow child to make choices about games, stories, and activities.
7. Have child dramatize simple stories.
8. Provide child with piggy bank and encourage naming coins as they are handled or dropped into bank.

READINGS

Carlson, B. W., and Ginglend, D. R.: Play activities for the retarded child, New York, 1961, Abingdon Press.

Currie, C.: Evaluating function of mentally retarded children through the use of toys and play activities, Amer. J. Occup. Ther. **23:**35-42, 1969.

Frank, L. K.: Motor patterns, play, and training in skills. In Falkner, F., editor: Human development, Philadelphia, 1966, W. B. Saunders Co.

Morgenstern, F. S.: Psychological handicaps in the play of handicapped children, Develop. Med. Child Neurol. **10:**115-120, 1968.

Smart, M. S., and Smart, R. C.: Children: development and relationships, New York, 1970, The Macmillan Co.

Wright, J. C.: Psychological development of the child. In Falkner, F., editor: Human development, Philadelphia, 1966, W. B. Saunders Co.

12

Discipline as an educational process

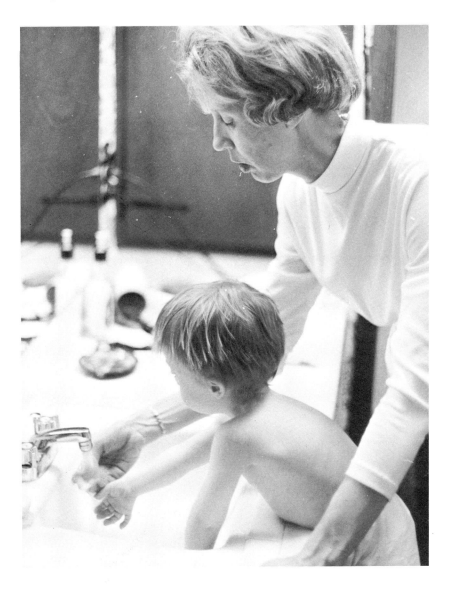

GENERAL CONCEPT

We want to help each child learn new social skills and overcome less mature behavior like wetting the bed, refusing to eat, throwing food, crawling rather than walking, sitting and rocking, sucking his thumb, attacking his peers or adults, having temper tantrums, refusing to brush his teeth, soiling himself after training has been established, etc. We want to help the child learn the things that will make him more acceptable to himself and others around him.

This is not easy, as any parent knows. Mothers frequently report that their children will not behave: "I've tried everything from being very kind, giving him everything he wants, spanking him, scolding him, bribing him, ridiculing him, taking away privileges, isolating him in his room, or distracting him by any means that I can think of at the time, and still I cannot get him to do the things I want."

Many parents do try everything, and in a very disorderly fashion. There is insufficient thought given to the goals appropriate for the child and inconsistency in what is prohibited or praised; often a method of discipline is rejected because it fails to work the first time it is tried. Parents often do not realize that discipline is an educational process, or should be so, and, as was noted in regard to the teaching of functional skills, appropriate expectations, consistency, and reinforcement are extremely important.

Frequently parents tend to rely heavily on punishment as a means of achieving discipline. Overuse of punishment can cause a child to feel that he is a failure and to expect failure in anything he may attempt. Obviously, such feelings in a retarded child work against the efforts of those around him to help him make the most of his abilities to discover and to learn.

A child faced with constant failure and punishment may well express his frustration in behavior that is much more disruptive than that for which he has been punished.

Moreover, punishment is sometimes quite ineffective in putting a stop to whatever the child was punished for. The cause of the behavior is apparently not affected by the punishment in such instances. It is not always possible to identify the cause of behavior, but we can assume that all behavior does have a cause.

The need for discrimination in the use of punishment is especially important for retarded children because they are slower to learn and to transfer knowledge from one situation to another.

Consistent limit setting works best and is most likely to result in learning in a highly structured situation such as when the mother is teaching table manners at the table, when dressing skills are being taught, or when toilet training is being carried out. In these situations the time and the setting direct the child's attention toward certain actions, and he is more likely to understand the limits set and the lesson to be learned.

A firm verbal reprimand can be as effective as a spanking. Its effectiveness is determined, however, by the amount of consistent warmth, praise, and affection that the child generally receives. Withdrawal of social approval is sufficiently effective punishment for a child to whom social approval has become meaningful. If a child is punished for behaving badly, the mother must remember, too, to praise him abundantly for behaving well.

Mentally retarded children have the same basic needs for love, social approval, acknowledgment of success, and feelings of trust and security that other children have, although they are often not as able to display them. The power of social approval that can be given immediately for some desirable behavior should be emphasized to parents. Approval means a smile, a thank you, a change in the quality or tone of voice, or a kiss or embrace. Tangible rewards such as candy, toys, money, gold stars, or points are also effective. Such concrete symbols in the possession of a child continue to remind him of his success.

The reward must be given as immediately as possible after the desired behavior occurs. In working with mentally retarded children, their short attention span must always be taken into account. Also, once certain actions of the child are decided on as "good" or "bad," it is of course important to be consistent in responding to them.

Many parents do not know how to make the most of rewards in teaching their children. Little Mary may be playing quietly and nicely for a while; mother is pleased and continues going about her duties. The next thing you know, Mary isn't being good and mother has to pay attention to some disruptive behavior, such as a tantrum. The point is that mothers are much more likely to pay attention when a child is naughty. The child may therefore find a certain amount of punishment "rewarding" just for the nearness or attention of the mother that comes with it. Instead of ignoring a child's good behavior, the mother should stop whatever she is doing to praise the child and give him a kiss or hug. Paying attention to a child when he is playing quietly or doing what you want him to do makes it less likely that the child will do something objectionable just to attract attention.

A child's interaction with siblings and other children is frequently the object of disciplinary action. Again, desirable responses of the child toward other children should always be praised and rewarded. Some aggressive behavior is natural, and if the child is being given the attention he needs, aggressiveness should be mild in degree and controllable through the systematic application of reinforcements.

The main features of healthy disciplinary practice seem to be emphasis on the educational nature of discipline, expectations that are appropriate for the child, consistent rewarding of desired behavior, and discriminate use of punishment within a general atmosphere of love and acceptance.

The suggested activities from the *Washington Guide* dealing with promoting sleep patterns in children, good discipline, and safety measures are presented in composite form and provide a basic framework that can be used in giving parents advice on general behavioral management in the home.

SUGGESTED ACTIVITIES FOR ENCOURAGING SLEEP

1 to 3 months
1. Provide separate sleeping arrangements away from your room.
2. Reduce noise and light stimulation when placing infant in bed.
3. Keep room at comfortable temperature with no drafts or extremes in heat.
4. Change position of crib in room occasionally.
5. Place child in different position from time to time for sleep.
6. Alternate from back to side to stomach.
7. Keep crib sides up.

4 to 8 months
1. Keep crib sides up.
2. Refrain from taking child into your room if he awakens.
3. Check to determine if there is cause for awakenings: hunger, teething, pain, cold, wet, noise, illness.
4. If baby-sitter is used, try to get a person infant knows. Explain bedtime and naptime arrangements to sitter.

9 to 12 months
1. Short crying periods may be source of tension release for child.
2. Observe him for signs of fatigue, irritability, or restlessness if naps or shorter.
3. Provide familiar person to baby-sit who knows his sleep routines.

4. Do not use bedtime or naptime as punishment.

13 to 18 months
1. Night terrors may be stopped by awakening child and offering reassurance.
2. Check to see that child is covered.
3. Avoid hazardous devices to keep child covered, including blanket clips, pins, and garments that enclose him to neck.

19 to 30 months
1. Arrange for quiet period of socialization prior to bedtime. Hold child, talk quietly with him, read to him, or tell story.
2. Ritualistic behavior may be present. For example, child may wish to arrange toys in certain way. You should allow child to carry out routine because it helps him overcome fear of unexpected or fear of dark.
3. Explain rituals to baby-sitter.
4. Allow child to take familiar toys or items to bed.
5. Allow crying-out period if he is safe, dry, and tucked in.
6. Place child in bed before he reaches excessive state of fatigue or excitement.
7. Eliminate sources of stimulation and fear.
8. Maintain consistent hour of bedtime.

31 to 48 months
1. TV programs may affect child's ability to go to sleep. Avoid violent programs.
2. Practice regularity and consistentcy to promote good sleeping habits.
3. Reassurance—use night-light or leave door ajar.

4. Encourage naps if child shows signs of fatigue or irritability.

49 to 52 months
1. Encourage napping if child is overly tired.
2. Explain to child if sitter will arrive after child is asleep.

SUGGESTIONS FOR HEALTHY DISCIPLINE AND SAFETY MEASURES IN RELATION TO AGE

1 to 3 months
1. a. Needs should be identified and met as promptly as possible.
   b. Every bit of fussing should not be interpreted as an emergency requiring immediate attention.
   c. Infant should not be ignored and permitted to cry for exhaustive periods, however.
2. Begin to present the discipline of having to wait so that infant can learn that tension and discomfort are bearable for short periods.
3. Place infant on surfaces that have sides to protect him from falling off.

4 to 8 months
1. a. Reserve "no-no" for when it is really needed.
   b. Be consistent with use of "no-no" in regard to activities and events that require it. Be friendly but firm.
2. Make special efforts to give attention to infant when he is quiet and amusing himself.
3. a. Introduce strangers into infant's environment gradually.
   b. Watch out for frightening situations with strangers during this stage.
   c. Play hiding games like peek-a-boo in which mother disappears and reappears.
   d. Allow infant to cling to mother and get used to people a little at a time.
   e. If baby-sitter is used, find person familiar to infant or introduce her

for brief periods before mother leaves infant in her care.
   f. Encourage gentle handling by mother, father, and siblings. Discourage rough handling, particularly by strangers.

9 to 12 months
1. a. Avoid setting unreasonable number of limits.
   b. Give simple commands one at a time.
   c. Allow time to conform to request.
   d. Gain child's attention before making request or giving command.
2. a. Begin setting and enforcing limits on where child is allowed to wander and explore.
   b. Remove tempting objects that could be dangerous or might be damaged.
   c. Be aware especially of sources of danger such as light sockets, protruding pot handles, hanging table covers, sharp objects, and hanging cords.
   d. Keep child away from fans and heaters, and don't place vaporizer close to infant's crib.
   e. Keep highchair at least 2 feet away from working and cooking surfaces in kitchen.
   f. Be certain that pans, basins, and tubs of hot water are never left unattended.
   g. Remove from floor, low cabinets, and under sink all possible poisons

or substances that are not food that can be eaten or drunk.

h. Keep child from objects or surfaces he may chew, e.g., porch rails, windowsills, and *repainted* toys or cribs, which may contain lead.

i. Instruct baby-sitter on all safety items.

3. Provide child with his own play objects and his own place for them.

4. a. Keep household poisons, cosmetics, pins, and buttons that he could put in his mouth out of his reach.

   b. Check toys for detachable small parts.

5. a. Once problem behaviors are defined, plan to work on changing only one behavior at a time until child behaves or conforms to expectations.

   b. Be certain that child understands old rules before adding new ones.

   c. Respond with consistency in enforcing old rules. Enforce each time; don't ignore next time.

   d. Provide regular pattern of mealtimes.

   e. Allow child to decide what he will eat and how much.

   f. Introduce new foods gradually over a period of time.

   g. Continue to offer foods that may have been rejected.

   h. Don't force food.

   i. Refrain from physically punishing child for changes in eating habits.

6. a. Provide regular time for naps and bedtime.

   b. Avoid excessive stimulation at bedtime or naptime.

   c. Ignore fussing and crying once safety and physical needs are satisfied and usual ritual is carried out.

   d. Keep child in his own room.

   e. Refrain from picking up and rocking and holding child if his needs seem satisfied.

13 to 18 months

1. a. Begin with one rule; add new ones as appropriate.

   b. In selecting new rules, choose rule on basis of being able to clearly define it to yourself and child, having it reasonable and enforceable at all times. Demand no more than fulfillment of defined expectations.

2. a. Immediately correct errors in behavior as they occur.

   b. Use consistent enforcement of short-term rules (which are given as verbal commands) and long-term rules (which pertain to chores and family routines).

   c. Ignore temper tantrums.

   d. Show child when you approve of his behavior, and praise him for obedience throughout day.

3. a. Set limits regarding play with doorknobs and car door handles.

   b. Keep him away from open unscreened windows. Latch screens.

   c. Supervise him around pools and ponds or drain or fence them.

   d. Lock medicine cabinets.

   e. Keep jars and bottles containing food, cosmetics, etc. out of reach.

   f. Use gate to protect child from falling down stairs.

19 to 30 months

1. a. Gain child's attention before giving simple commands, one at a time. Praise him for success.

   b. Add new rules as child conforms to old ones.

   c. Refrain from expecting immediate obedience.

2. Set up alternatives from which child can choose for such matters as what he will wear that day, which game to play, which reward he will receive.

3. Make special efforts to answer questions. Give simple explanations. Gauge need for simplifying by number of times act is repeated or question asked.

4. a. Supervise on stair rails and waxed floors.
   b. Set rules about crossing streets and carrying knives, sharp objects, or glass objects.
   c. Have outdoor play area securely fenced or supervised.
   d. When riding in car, secure child safely by seat belt or insist on his sitting in back seat. Do not permit standing on car seats.
   e. Keep matches out of reach.
   f. Shield adult tools such as knives, lawnmowers, and sharp tools.
5. Practice consistency in responding to behavior.
6. a. If new child is expected, explain verbally and through play.
   b. When new baby arrives, set special times aside for exclusive attention to older child and exercise more patience with him.
   c. Allow child to help with care of new sibling.

31 to 48 months
1. a. Exercise consistency in parental demands. Enforce each time.
   b. Give immediate recognition and approval for acceptable behavior.
   c. Refrain from use of threats that produce fearfulness. Refrain from constant reprimands.
   d. Denial of privileges should not be excessive or prolonged.
2. a. Give simple explanations. Allow child chance to demonstrate understanding by talking about an event, situation, or rule.
   b. Eliminate unnecessary and impractical rules.
   c. Choices should be offered, particularly in problem areas.
3. a. Assign simple household tasks that child can carry out each day. Show approval for performance and success.
   b. Decide if child is capable of doing what is asked by observing him.
   c. Determine how much time child

seems to need to complete chore or activity before setting time limit.
4. a. Be extra cautious in supervising tricycle riding near streets and driveways.
   b. Don't permit child to dash into street while playing.
   c. Areas under swings and slides should not be paved.
   d. Be an example to child, e.g., don't jaywalk.
   e. Provide scissors that are blunt tipped.

49 to 52 months
1. Give child more opportunities to be independent.
2. Use simple explanations and reasoning.
3. Ask child to define rule if he disobeys, to see if he understands rule.
4. Have child correct mistakes as they occur.
5. Don't punish without previous warnings.
6. Praise for successful performance.
7. Use gold stars on chart for rewards.
8. Avoid making promises that can't always be kept.
9. Avoid bribing, ridicule, shaming, teasing, inflicting pain, and using unfavorable comparison with other children.
10. Provide appropriate models of behavior for his imitation (parents, brothers, sisters, neighborhood child, or maybe TV hero).
11. If you will be leaving for social obligation, vacation, etc., let child know well beforehand.
12. Be more patient and give more time to conform and more approval for desirable behavior at times of stress such as illness or accident, moving into new neighborhood, separation from friends, death of someone close to child, divorce of the parents, or hospitalization of child or parent.

The following case represents an illustration of many of the concepts and the rationale outlined in this text. One of the primary problems in the family was discipline of the retarded child. The child and parents were seen by an interdisciplinary team in which nursing had a significant role to play in management.

CASE ILLUSTRATION: EVALUATION AND COMPREHENSIVE CARE OF A PRESCHOOL-AGED CHILD WHO IS MENTALLY RETARDED

Janie was seen for evaluation by an interdisciplinary team at a mental retardation clinic when she was 31 months of age. Her parents had been referred to the clinic by the state school for the retarded. They had inquired there about finding resources to help them care for Janie.

The nuclear family included the father, 34 years of age, a high school graduate, a car salesman, and in good health and the mother, 32 years of age, a registered nurse, working part-time, whose general health was good.

Her history of pregnancies was as follows: 1959—healthy boy; 1962—spontaneous abortion; 1963—Janie; and 1966—healthy boy.

The oldest boy had demonstrated some behavior problems both at home and at school. He had difficulty learning how to read. The school personnel told the parents that he would learn if he just applied himself.

There were no other abnormalities in terms of behavior, physical status, or health development in the immediate family.

Pregnancy and delivery

The mother was 29 years of age at the time Janie was conceived. She initiated prenatal care during the second month. She was hospitalized for several weeks during the second month for high blood pressure, edema, and headaches. She had no proteinuria, convulsions, nausea, or vomiting. She was given diuretics and phenobarbital. During the last trimester, she had a systolic pressure of 190. She noted less fetal activity during the entire pregnancy as compared to her other pregnancies.

The delivery was uneventful, no induction was used, labor was three hours, and the child was a vertex presentation. She cried immediately, and respirations were good. Her birth weight was 5 pounds 5 ounces, and she was 18 3/4 inches in length. The parents knew a few hours after birth that she was not a normal child and had characteristics of Down's syndrome. The grandmother was extremely upset by this and made the mother promise not to tell their friends that there was anything abnormal about Janie. The grandmother insisted that she was normal.

Neonatal history

Janie had features of Down's syndrome, particularly epicanthal folds. She had a good sucking reflex and regained her birth weight at 1 week of age. The pediatrician and the parents noticed that the child was rather limp when held. In addition, they noted minimal activity on the part of the child. She cried less than the other children.

Infancy

In relation to motor development, Janie rolled over at 5 months, sat without support at 12 months, walked without support at 26 months, and went upstairs at 27 months of age. In respect to feeding, she took no solids until 9 months of age. She had difficulty swallowing. This may have been because of her large tongue. Her appetite was generally poor. The parents reported babbling at 8 months of age.

She has had chronic and constant upper respiratory infections and rhinitis. There was frequent clear, yellow, thick nasal drainage. Her six-month well-baby checkup revealed iron-deficiency anemia. She was given three intramuscular injections of iron. She has had roseola but no other childhood diseases. There has been a constant problem with diaper rash.

Physical examination—significant findings

Body proportions: Brachycephaly, with short limbs
Eyes: Brushfield spots, epicanthal folds
Cardiovascular system: Pulses regular, heart sounds normal, no murmur
Extremities: Normal symmetry; Hands spadelike; short incurving of fifth finger, with rudimentary second phalanx; broken palmar crease; wide space between big and second toe; joints show increased range of motion

Psychological examination

This child was compliant and functioned very well on an early level of behavior in which response to things is required. Her response to language, however, was poor. She obtained a developmental quotient of 53. Her developmental age was 16.4 months at the actual age of 30.8 months. This placed the child in the moderately retarded range.

Speech and hearing evaluation

Janie was responsive to the examiner and to toys that were presented. She responded by babbling, smiling, and playing as a normal infant would do. She manipulated blocks in and out of the box, loved a doll, rolled a ball, and pretended to eat with a spoon. On the Meekin Verbal Language Development Scale, she obtained a year level of 0.86. The impression was that there was a moderate language delay. It was recommended that the book *Teaching Your Child to Talk,* by Dr. Charles Van Riper, be used to encourage language stimulation at home.

Family evaluation

The parents were seen separately by the social worker and psychiatrist. They were judged to be mature, intelligent, and well-adjusted persons; however, they were having definite problems. These revolved around their feelings toward their child with Down's syndrome and her handling. The parents demonstrated general disagreement about how to handle discipline for all the children, as well as Janie, the father feeling that one should be extremely strict. He advocated physical punishment. The mother tended to be overly permissive to compensate for the father's behavior. She did not approve of physical punishment.

Nursing evaluation

The mother was seen as seeking resources for teaching the child. In terms of self-help skills, Janie finger-fed herself, was learning to use a spoon, had hand-mouth coordination, and could scoop with the spoon but spilled when placing it in her mouth. She was not toilet trained and wore diapers. She pulled off buttons instead of manipulating them to unbutton. She could open and close a zipper, unsnap her pajamas, and remove her shoes and stockings along with clothes that did not have buttons on them.

She was entertained by noisemaking toys. She enjoyed pulling toys for the noise and watching toys that moved. She delighted in banging toys together. She placed all toys and objects in her mouth. Her chief companion at play was the 14-month-old sibling. One of the behavior problems at the time was her destructive behavior. She had a short attention span. For example, if left alone, she would get into things and climb onto almost anything. She did not respond to the word "no" and did not seem to understand explanations. The mother had tried disciplining her by removing objects or diverting her attention without much success. When she could not get what she wanted, she often resorted to severe temper tantrums, screamed, struck at people, stamped her feet, and threw objects. The parents disagreed considerably in the handling of these episodes; the mother was not willing to punish her, whereas the father felt that some punishment was necessary. He did not become involved in the child's discipline.

Nutritional evaluation

The diet was determined to be essentially adequate in nutrients. The mother was concerned because Janie did not chew meat and did not seem to like the texture of meat. The hemoglobin was low, and the child demonstrated pallor. Suggestions included encouraging self-feeding and encouraging chewing with foods other than meat, initially. Suggestions were oven-dried toast, lettuce, raw crisp apple, and stringless celery. It was suggested that the mother beat an egg into a patty of ground meat. A meat patty was one meat-type food that Janie liked. Soup was to be fortified with beef juices. There was no pressure to get meat, as such, into the child's diet.

Case management

As the team members conferenced this case, it became evident that Janie did have many of the symptoms of Down's syndrome and was moderately retarded. This the family knew before the evaluation, but they appreciated the interpretation of these findings by the clinic team. They were particularly interested in what this might mean in terms of Janie's development ten to fifteen years hence.

One of their immediate concerns was how they could manage Janie better; therefore it was decided that the most immediate need was to help with management of behavior. The team had seen and heard evidence that there was disagreement about managing the child's behavior. Why were the parents at odds concerning this? Was this peculiar to their management of Janie and not the other children? These questions were to be answered through continued contact with the family. The public health nurse planned to observe the interactions that took place between Janie and her mother to get a clearer picture of the behavior problems of concern to the parents and team members. These observations were to be made during a series of home visits.

As opportunities were presented to the parents to discuss their concerns, they began to reveal how little they had communicated their feelings about Janie to each other. The mother symbolized the child as an "angel." Her own mother's admonition at the time of the child's birth had led her to be protective of Janie. She could not perceive her as doing wrong. In addition, how can you spank an "angel?" The father expressed concern for his wife's health. Janie was such a behavior problem that all his wife had time for was to pick up after the children. He could not understand why his wife did not discipline Janie. The mother felt that she had to be permissive because her husband tended to be extremely strict with the children. However, he did not punish Janie.

At this time, it became appropriate for the nurse to begin discussing with the mother the possibility of using some techniques of reinforcement therapy. The mother was receptive to discussing learning, behavior, and ways to respond more effectively to Janie. She was aware of the need for observations and the possibility of becoming involved in a behavioral modification program. She was told that it might take additional time on her part but that the team was willing to work with her if she wanted. Two home visits were made for this type of discussion and to make a general assessment of the home environment. It was decided that mornings from about 10 to 12 were the best times to collect behavioral observations. It was stressed that she should go on with her activities as usual because it was important to see behaviors as they normally occurred.

A half-hour sample of the recording of random behaviors follows. These recordings were categorized with respect to inappropriate behaviors, appropriate behaviors, and the mother's attending. The mean response in two one-hour samples of behavior with respect to appropriate-inappropriate behaviors and whether or not the mother attended to them is presented here. It was evident that the mother was attending mainly to the inappropriate behaviors. However, in spite of this, the child had a high percentage of appropriate behavior that the mother was not noticing.

Categorization of behaviors and attention

Behaviors		Attending	Nonattending
Total behaviors	81	19	62
Appropriate	51	6	45
Inappropriate	30	13	17

10:45   Mother is folding clothes. Janie pulls the aerial on the TV set back and forth. She goes to mother and holds the radio up; mother rewinds the radio so that it makes noise. Brother is in the room with a caterpillar toy.

10:58   Janie watches mother put clothes in the basket. Mother says, "What do you have in your mouth?" Janie wanders over to the dining chest. Doesn't take anything off. Goes into the kitchen, tries to get mother's purse. Can't get the purse. Jim, her brother, takes a plastic tree off the table. Janie grabs the other half of the tree. He gives it to her. Mother picks Janie up. "How much do you have in your mouth?"

11:09   Mother tells Janie to come, picks her up, and brings her upstairs. Mother goes back to folding clothes. Janie comes downstairs. She talks to Jim, goes with her brother into the playroom, and goes up the stairs. Mother gets the children down. Mother carries Janie after getting downstairs. Janie runs into the parents' room, where she goes behind the dresser. Mother says, "I know she's into something," finds her with the alarm clock, and picks her up. "I'll wring your neck; don't you do that"; then she kisses her.

11:15   Janie is playing with a screw toy. She gets up, makes some babbling noises, ba-ba, clicks her tongue, goes into the playroom, and starts climbing the steps. Jim starts to follow. Both children go upstairs and stay there for two minutes. Mother going to get them. "I'm not going to chase you," mother says. "Mother's not going to look at you." Mother brings Janie downstairs. "I've a feeling you don't plan on staying down here. That's John's toy. Can't have this." Mother picks her up, kisses her.

11:22   Mother rubs Janie's back, lets her down. Janie goes back upstairs. Sits on stairs. John is upstairs doing puzzles. Comes back down the stairs, takes away whistle from brother, goes into living room. Janie on stairs. "Get down, get down," says mother. Mother lifts her down.

The appropriate behaviors were considered as any play behaviors, watching the mother, and going from one room to another. Inappropriate behaviors consisted of pulling objects off tables and window shelves, taking things out of drawers, and breaking things. The mother's attention consisted of looking at Janie, touching her, or talking to her.

After the data had been categorized, the nurse went over it with the mother. She was silent at first and then responded, "She never really does anything. I often wonder if she will ever learn how to accomplish anything—like when she's older." The nurse picked up this cue and remarked that Janie did not have many play behaviors and maybe this would be the place to start. The types of play activities that Janie would enjoy were discussed—such things as playing with dolls, mirror play, and dressing in the mother's old clothes and shoes. It was stressed that it was better for Janie to have just one or two play objects at a time and that they should be available in an environment conducive to play. There happened to be a room in the house that was not being used that the mother was encouraged to use as the playroom.

On the following visit, it was observed that the mother had had her husband repair her own childhood doll furniture. There was a doll and some old clothes and shoes. Most of the visit was spent in the playroom. As long as the nurse stayed in the playroom, the mother stayed, and as long as the mother stayed, Janie stayed. There was gradual interaction between the nurse and Janie and between the mother and Janie, such as gaining her attention and interest in rocking, dressing, and feeding the doll, helping her dress in the old clothes, etc. Initially the time spent in the playroom was approximately forty-five minutes. During this time the nurse pointed out to the mother the child's increasing interest in play. At times when the mother needed to leave the room, Janie followed, illustrating to the mother how influential her attention was on Janie's behavior.

The next five visits were spent almost entirely in the playroom. After this the length of time spent in the playroom during a visit was gradually decreased. It was observed that the child had some play maintenance behavior without the mother in the room. This gradually increased. Observations two months after the program was initiated demonstrated that the mother was attending to more of the appropriate behaviors. There were no recorded inappropriate behaviors in the two one-hour time samples.

As the mother began paying attention to more appropriate behavior, she also seemed able to begin putting limits on inappropriate behavior. She was able to slap the child's hand or bottom. As evidenced by her response, the word "no" began to take on meaning to the child. Although there was no systematic observation of the mother's interactions with the other children, it appeared that she managed the other children more appropriately.

REFERENCES

Bijou, S. W., and Baer, D. M.: Child development: a systematic and empirical theory, vol. I, New York, 1961, Appleton-Century-Crofts.

Ginott, H. G.: Between parent and child: new solutions to old problems, New York, 1969, Avon Books.

Jensen, G. D.: The well child's problems: management in the first six years, Chicago, 1962, Year Book Medical Publishers, Inc.

Patterson, G. R., and Gullion, M. E.: Living with children: new methods for parents and teachers, Champaign, Ill., 1968, Research Press.

summary

The major points that have been repeatedly emphasized throughout this text for meeting the special learning needs of the handicapped child are the following:

1. Consider the parents' motivation and readiness to carry out a teaching plan.
2. Consider the physical, physiological, and neurological factors that indicate the child's readiness to learn a task.
3. Set realistic goals based on this assessment.
4. Identify the component steps of a learning task and work to achieve small goals that lead to larger goals.
5. Progress from simple to complex tasks.
6. Use a system of recording progress.
7. Secure and maintain the attention of the child.
8. Clearly demonstrate expectations to the child.
9. Provide specific cues to which he can attend.
10. Positively reinforce each new step accomplished by the child by immediately rewarding him. Avoid inadvertent reinforcement of negative behavior.
11. Provide for the child's repeated practice of learning experiences.
12. Be supportive to parents as they adapt to changes that are occurring in their child.

appendix

Developmental assessment tools
for nurses*

The past ten years has been characterized by a significant increase in interest and activities related to the overall problem of mental deficiency. In spite of this progressive movement in many areas, there has been a significant lag in the development of techniques and procedures for accurate identification and assessment of delayed development in infants and preschool children. This is not meant to discredit the psychologists who have at their disposal a vast repertoire of standardized intelligence tests. However, the lack of qualified psychologists is as disturbing as the personnel situation in nursing. It is not uncommon to find many health departments, pediatric wards and clinics, schools, head-start programs, and other such agencies without a qualified psychologist. Yet these are the very settings in which children are often first seen by a professional person. Medicine recognized this problem forty years ago, which resulted in the creation of the Gesell Developmental Schedules, a tool which is still widely used by physicians in practice today. The public health or pediatric nurse, however, who in many settings holds the unique position of having the most, and often the first, contact with a child, still remains relatively uninvolved in developmental screening and assessment on a systematic basis. It is hoped that this afternoon's sessions will enable us to make better use of the available tools, as well as motivate us toward developing better tools of screening and assessment.

HISTORICAL OVERVIEW

The study of child development as we know it today is a relatively new scientific endeavor. This is hardly surprising when one considers society's views

---

*From Pesek, Sharon: Developmental assessment tools for nurses. In Proceedings of the Fourth Annual Workshop, Nursing in Mental Retardation Programs, University of Miami, 1967, sponsored by Children's Bureau, U.S. Department of Health, Education, and Welfare and Child Development Center. Used by permission.

of children down through the ages. Although Plato gave some recognition to the fact that children possessed individual differences, for the most part, children were looked upon as miniature versions of adults until well into the nineteenth century. Children and adults were expected to share equally in work loads, and child-rearing methods emphasized conformity of the child's behavior to that of the adult's. Corresponding to the social concept of the "miniature adult" was the religious doctrine of original sin. In this frame of reference, education was primarily geared toward "making over" the innately evil child to prepare him to live in the more righteous world of the hereafter. Compounding the problems of child rearing during this time were the astonishing birth mortality rates and the prevalence of death and disease, all making for extremely short life expectancies. With doctors spending most of their time saving children's lives and teachers emphasizing their preparation for better things to come, not to mention the psychologists who were just beginning to distinguish themselves as a discipline apart from philosophy, it is hardly surprising that there was little interest or concern with the study of child development.

Biology actually provided the impetus for subsequent study of the developing child through the contributions of Darwin's evolutionary concepts. From Darwin's thesis that human life had evolved from lower animal forms, the psychologists of the late nineteenth century deducted that a child reenacts the evolution of the human species in the growth and development sequence. This concept was termed "recapitulation." It became the basic thesis of G. Stanley Hall, who is considered the founder of child psychology in the United States. Hall and his associates at Clark University, including such psychologists of later eminence as Gesell and Terman, conducted many studies on the behavior, interests, and abilities of children. Hall's enthusiastic interest spread rapidly, and by the turn of the century many associations for child study, as well as individual investigators, had joined the bandwagon.

The first actual studies of child development were biographical in nature, in that they were based on an investigator's observations of a single child, at times a son or daughter. Piaget's extensive studies are representative of this type. While these studies are now recognized as being biased and limited in general application, they were nonetheless invaluable, for they brought out the need for more critical evaluation and refined methods, as well as recognizing the importance of childhood study per se.

Assessment of child development became a concern in the early 1900's. The phrase "mental test" was first used by Cattell in 1893. Binet's influential work followed Cattell's. Among Binet's many contributions were the grouping of developmental tasks into age levels and the use of the term "mental age." The early testing movement was rounded out in 1916 by Terman, who introduced the term "intelligence quotient," which, for better or worse, has remained with us since.

The twentieth century has been one of furious activity in many areas, not the least of which has been child psychology. The numerous theories and investigations related to child development during the past sixty years have evolved into three major viewpoints—specifically, the behavioral, the psycho-analytic, and the maturational schools of thought. These viewpoints are actually more sophisticated and refined statements of the old "heredity vs. environment" argument. Each theoretical framework has explained the child's development in a different way, and each has had an impact on the child-rearing customs of the times. Their influence has also been reflected in the numerous tests and assessment tools which have evolved, as well as the lay public's increasing concern with developmental norms, IQs, and so forth. A brief review of the three major movements in child psychology will serve to illustrate the influences they have exerted.

The behaviorist movement, under the leadership of John B. Watson, was an outgrowth of John Locke's "tabula rasa" concept. This concept encompasses the view that emotions and behavior are shaped primarily by the learning opportunities experienced by the infant; little credit is given to the influence of heredity or innate characteristics. The innate units of behavior that Watson did allow were termed reflexes. He hypothesized that complex behavior was constructed from these simple behavior units through association and condi-tioning. These views came to be known as the "social learning" theory, with its practical application being manifested by such child-rearing customs as "timed-feedings" and encouragement of early responsibility and independence in the child. The soundness of Watson's theories, which were based upon experimental animal studies, has accounted for their sustained popularity. Recently, the social learning theory has been recognized as having extensive application in teaching self-help skills and eradicating negative behavior of both retardates and emo-tionally disturbed children. Watson's original concepts formed the foundation of modern operant learning theory.

Soon after Watson's theories became known, Arnold Gesell, in his observations of infant behavior, repeatedly observed developmental phenomena which he felt could not be satisfactorily explained in terms of the social learning theory. Gesell's studies of infant behavior led him to conclude that the impetus for much of the infant's behavior is inborn and that certain developmental phenomena occur in an orderly sequence without any direct influence from external stimuli or manipulation. Gesell did allow that the child could certainly profit from practice and stimulation, but the initiating force for certain developmental tasks was internal. Gesell termed this internally regulated concept of development the "maturational" theory. Support for Gesell's theory was found in a number of studies. Ames recorded the behavior of infants through movies and noted that new and complex behavior often appeared for the first time in a form so complete that the proficiency of these skills was not changed significantly after several months of practice of the particular skill.[1] Current research related to imprinting in the field of ethology has also provided evidence for this viewpoint.

Gesell's theories on child development and child-rearing practices have been widely disseminated through his prolific writings, with which we are all familiar. Perhaps more important than his advice to parents, however, is the data he collected on child development, which he formulated into the well-known Gesell Developmental Schedules. These will be discussed later, along with other current testing material. For the present, it is important to bear in mind that for all of the criticism and controversy Gesell's theories have raised, he did call attention to the innate factors in infant behavior, as well as establish beginning data on the developmental sequence as it is accepted today. Most important, perhaps, was Gesell's recognition that medical examinations of newborns could not be limited to the stimulus-response approach traditionally used in the neurological examination. He advocated eliciting the baby's active participation in order to observe as many behaviors as possible. Thus he originated the concept of systematic developmental assessment of infants and preschool children.

Another major influence upon modern child psychology has been the work of Sigmund Freud, the founder of psychoanalysis. As we all know, Freud's work with neurotic adult patients led to the formulation of his theories on personality development and indicated the crucial role of childhood experiences on subsequent personality maladjustment. It would be impossible to condense Freud's maxims to a few sentences, but essentially he said that personality development progresses through a sequence of stages—oral, anal, oedipal—and that experiences during each period inevitably affect character and behavior traits in later life.

We are all inescapably familiar with psychoanalytic influences on child-rearing customs, as well as their contributions to personality assessment. It is only recently that psychoanalytic theory has exerted its influence on the process of intellectual assessment. Psychologists have always astutely observed that much more information could be obtained in a testing situation than a mere IQ score. However, as long as psychologists were busy debating whether intelligence was innately or environmentally determined, the emotional component of testing behavior received little attention. In 1946, long after Freud's initial publications, Rappaport and his associates began to analyze test performances in terms of psychoanalytic thought. For example, they theorized that arithmetic and memory (digit span) subtests made demands on the ego functions of attention and concentration.[16] Rappaport's theory, in essence, combined intellectual and personality functioning into one theoretical framework. Variation in intellectual functioning was thought to be related to the quality of underlying thought processes. Subsequent studies concerned with the relationship between impulsiveness and intellectual performance have supported this view of intellectual functioning which relates affect, innate drives, and intellectual activity in the same theoretical framework. The culmination of this trend was a publication by Fromm in 1954 which provided a theoretical analysis of the Stanford-Binet in terms of psychoanalytic psychology.[12]

While the three major theories continue to flourish, with more objective data being obtained all the time, the dominant thinking among most of the child-related professions leans toward integration. It is recognized that these theories are not necessarily contradictory or mutually exclusive. To quote a recent review, "All are concerned with learning, with the interaction of organism and environment. They all highlight different facets of behavior, and use different conceptual systems. And, undoubtedly, they are all a little bit right."[7]

CURRENT TEST AND ASSESSMENT SCALES

The increase in activity in the field of child psychology since the turn of the century has been accompanied by the development of a multitude of intelligence tests and developmental scales. As tools were tried and tested on a longitudinal basis, it became evident that measures of infant intellignece had little correlation with intelligence scores of school-age children. Intelligence tests for older children were based largely on language-related items, which could only be measured to a limited extent in infants. Psychologists began to wonder if there was such a thing as infant "intelligence." Nancy Bayley pointed out that infant intelligence tests were devised and standardized on the assumption that maturation in sensorimotor function and simple adaptation are intellectual and should be predictive of later intelligence performance. She observed, however, that these functions had low correlations with "adult intelligence."[4] It is now recognized that most infant tests are really developmental schedules or standardized ways of observing infants' behavior as compared with "normal" infant behavior. Since there are only so many behaviors that can be observed in infants, many of the developmental scales used today bear close resemblance to one another. Our concern today is with those tools that can best be used by nurses to assess the developmental level of infants and preschool children.

In evaluating any developmental assessment tool, there are certain considerations to be kept in mind. To use any tool, one should understand its purpose. This may sound elementary, but throughout the child-related professions, screening tests and developmental scales are often used as the basis for such tasks as predicting future intellectual functioning, assessing adaptability, and making medical diagnoses. Ability to predict intellectual functioning is a major need among the professionals working with children today, consequently, many investigators have tried to devise infant and preschool tests that would serve this purpose. With regard to this purpose, psychologists agree that infant scales are unsatisfactory for prediction when used for infants under 15 months. Exceptions to this have been demonstrated but usually with limited samples. While the problem of predictability does not relate directly to the nurse's needs, it is nonetheless important to be aware of the controversy surrounding it. A second consideration in evaluating an assessment tool is that it should conform to the criteria of a good assessment tool. The criteria will depend to some extent upon the purpose for which the assessment tool is used, but some criteria are applicable to tests in general.

First, the test should have some degree of reliability, that is, give the same results when used by different people. Second, the test should have validity or the ability to obtain approximately the same scores when given at different times. This means that the test should be able to predict later functioning, which as already stated, is not as applicable to infant and preschool tests as other criteria. A third consideration is the standardization process, or the population from which the test's norms are derived. Knobloch and associates have emphasized that developmental scales used by physicians should be able to test the patterns of behavior in which neurological abnormality occurs.[20] She also stresses the importance of small age intervals so that children of all ages can be assessed accurately.[19] Ruess and co-workers define a developmental screening tool as one that allows a large number of children to be screened for developmental delay in a relatively short amount of time. He adds to the above criteria those qualities necessary for a good screening tool, which include (1) short administration time, (2) minimum of testing equipment, (3) inclusion of as wide a variety of developmental functions associated with "intelligence" as possible (that is, language, adaptive behavior), (4) significant correlation of test with a more valid intelligence test, for example, Stanford-Binet, and (5) proficient use of instrument to be learned with a minimum of experience by a child specialist with no previous psychometric training[27] With respect to these criteria, let us now look at some of the developmental assessment tools that might lend themselves to use by nurses.

The Gesell Developmental Schedules were produced at the Yale Clinic of Child

Development following an extensive series of investigations on 107 "normal" infants. The "test" is a clinical appraisal of an infant's behavior in each of four areas, including motor (gross and fine), adaptive, language, and personal-social, as compared with characteristic behavior of normal children. The infant's behavior in each area is expressed by a developmental age which is then converted to a developmental quotient. The test procedure is illustrated and explained in Gesell's 1954 publication, *Developmental Diagnosis.*[13]

The original Developmental Schedules were established in 1925, but these have undergone considerable refinement and revision since their first appearance. The most significant research related to the Gesell studies has been done by Knobloch and Pasamanick. In their writings they emphasize Gesell's maturational theory; that is, that development is an orderly process with later behavior predictable from behavior observed at an earlier age. They have done extensive studies to support this, encompassing many areas of functioning. For example, they have indicated that abnormal feeding behavior, abnormal startle reflexes, excessive crying, sucking difficulty, vomiting, and other abnormal behaviors observed as early as 1 month have a significant correlation with abnormal neurological and developmental examinations at 40 weeks. Such behaviors as irritability, hyperactivity, perseveration, and short attention span at the three-year examination were observed in a large number of those children who had presented abnormal behavior at 40 weeks. They have concluded that the Gesell Schedules are helpful in diagnosing brain damage because of the abnormal neurological patterns revealed through the test.[20]

Evaluation of the Gesell Developmental Schedules as an assessment tool is divided into two schools of thought, namely the physicians and the psychologists. According to the 1965 *Mental Measurements Yearbook,*[6] enthusiasm for the Gesell tests continues to run high among physicians. From the viewpoint of the psychologists, however, the Gesell Developmental test is far from satisfactory. They allow that Gesell's observations were invaluable contributions to the study of child development, but as to the test itself, it is described by Anastasi as "relatively crude."[2]

Major criticisms of the Gesell Scale have centered around its failure to meet the qualifications of a good psychological test. With respect to standardization, Gesell's normative sample was too small (107 children). It was not representative of the general population, as all of the children came from the middle class socioeconomic group, with education and occupation of parents similar. Nancy Bayley has stated that the homogeneity of Gesell's sample explains his convictions about the consistency of development in all children. She feels that had his sample been more diverse, he would have concluded that infant behavior is highly irregular and unpredictable in reference to the total population.[5] Other criticisms are aimed at the low correlation of Gesell tests with standardized intelligence tests given at a later age. Several studies utilizing Gesell's test[10, 17] have found it to be of little predictive value when given to infants under 16 months. Knobloch and her associates have reported a correlation of .51 between tests given at 40 weeks and again at 3 years. Interestingly enough, the highest correlations between early and later tests have been with subnormal children, both on the Gesell and other infant scales. [10, 19]

A final criticism of the Gesell test is related to the disproportionate use of test items. For example, the scale at 44 to 48 weeks includes no language items, with relatively few adaptive items at 48 weeks. Considering the above, one would have to conclude that the Gesell is not appropriate as an infant intelligence scale, nor is it usually regarded as one. It can, however, give us important information and observations about the present position of a child with respect to developmental expectations. Its use as a screening device might be limited to those clinics that have a small population demanding testing at any one time, although many of the items can be administered in connection with the physical examination. Certainly a working knowledge of the Gesell would be valuable, as many subsequent tests have been based on the developmental tasks found in his Developmental Schedules.

Perhaps more appropriate for purposes of sereening is Knobloch's and Pasamanick's Developmental Screening Inventory, which is based on Gesell's Schedules. The items are similar to those in Gesell's test, but they have been reduced in number, having demonstrated that results from the abbreviated screening inventory correlate with those of the full developmental evaluation.[19]

The format of the D. S. I. is a useful one, with a unique feature being the alloted space for serial recordings of test results. The inclusion of definitive criteria for the passing of particular items is helpful, particularly to those examiners who are unfamiliar with the finer points of behavioral and neurological assessment. Because the test is almost identical to the original Gesell Schedules in terms of age placement of items, distribution of items, and so forth, it is subject to the same criticisms outlined in the discussion of Gesell's test. In spite of this, the correlations obtained both in terms of reliability and validity are impressive, although the sample of children used to support predictability of the test is rather small, being only 66.[19] We are also given no data on the subjects in terms of socioeconomic levels, parental education and occupation, and so forth, all of which enter into the developmental achievements as reflected in standardized intelligence tests. Another problem seems to be in the ability of untrained examiners (medical students) to administer, score, and interpret the test. While this is explained by the authors in terms of lack of motivation, it is somewhat disturbing to find that two fifths of the administered test results in the pilot study were unsatisfactory for "technical" reasons. Considering all these factors, an infant test which is able to identify later neurological and intellectual functioning in 95% of the cases is certainly a significant contribution to the available screening devices.

The Cattell Infant Intelligence Scale is the infant test regarded most highly by the psychologists. This scale covers an age range from 2 to 30 months and has incorporated many of the Gesell items. Cattell's objective was to improve upon previous scales, which he attempted to do by (1) eliminating items in the "personal-social area" which he felt were influenced by home training, (2) providing more equal distribution of items over the age ranges covered, and (3) providing more refined age scaling. He also constructed the test so that it constituted a downward extension of the Stanford-Binet, intermingling Stanford-Binet items with the infant items from the 22-month level on, so as to create one continuous scale from infancy to maturity. While this is certainly helpful to the psychologist, the nurse and physician who are unfamiliar with the Stanford-Binet may find other tests more appropriate. Part of the physicians' and nurses' lack of enthusiasm for the Cattell may be explained by the fact that its use has not been included in their training. Before disregarding it as a useful tool, however, it should be kept in mind that the Cattell Scales show some of the highest correlations between early and later testing of any of the available tests in children past the age of 9 months.[2, 17]

The Bayley Scales, developed by Nancy Bayley around 1930, are primarily of historical significance. Her scale consisted of 186 behaviors ranging from 1 month to 3 years of age. The test-retest correlations of her tests were so low that she concluded the "intelligence behavior" of infants was very different from later adult "intelligence."[4] Since that time, she has undertaken revision and restandardization of her scales, which are to be published in the future.

The Vineland Social Maturity Scale is a schedule used to assess an individual's ability to look after his practical needs and to take responsibility. The test covers a range from birth to 25 years but has been found to be most useful in the preschool and school-age years. The desired information is obtained through an interview with an informant or the subject himself and essentially reflects what the subject actually does in his daily living routine. Through using the Vineland in our clinic in conjunction with other standardized intelligence tests, we have found it to be a useful tool for assessing possible management problems. It is also helpful in gauging a child's readiness and adjustment to various situations, that is, school, institutionalization, and so forth. It also may be a valuable, but certainly not comprehensive, tool around which nursing interviews are structured. In comparing Vineland Scores to other tests, we have noted the presence of a positive bias when parents serve as Vineland informants, which usually accounts for approximately a ten-point increase in score. An additional problem with the Vineland is that the Social Quotient provides a global estimate of functioning which does not reflect the specific strengths and weaknesses as measured by the eight Vineland categories. Thus the use of a single score may penalize a physically handicapped child whose physical disabilities may interfere with such items as locomotion. It has also been noted that some items reflect cultural or socioeconomic differences in child-rearing customs or opportunities, that is, those dealing with wandering about the neighborhood alone or using money. These, too, may tend to distort the score. In addition, many items are not applicable to institutionalized subjects.

A recent addition to the roster of developmental tests is the Denver Developmental Screening Test. With regard to criteria for a good screening tool, this seems to be an excellent test. The normative sample is adequate as well as representative of the population. Developmental norms are given for various parental occupation groups, which allow a child to be tested relative to the cultural group in which he is reared. The format of the test is unique in that it allows one to get a quick visual picture of the child's strengths and weaknesses in each of four areas. Because it points up deficit areas, it allows teachers and nurses to concentrate on these in their training programs. The test is concise enough to lend itself to screening purposes, with age intervals close enough to give a fairly refined estimate of functioning. The questionnaire which is filled out by the parent gives valuable background information important to referral sources. One of the few weaknesses of the test lies in its dependence on parental report for many of the items. While it is recognized that a screening situation may not be conducive to observing all items, the reported items may tend to distort the score. On the whole, it appears that this test may supply a much needed tool, and I am sure we are all eager to learn more about it.

In addition to the above tests, many tests based on single tasks such as drawing or block stacking are available.[28] Considering the doubtful validity of the more comprehensive developmental assessment tools, there are even more objections to using single test items as a basis for global assessment. This applies to form-boards, drawing tests, and vocabulary tests when used alone to determine mental age. Even as a screening device, these single tests are misleading. This is not to say they cannot contribute information about the child, particularly his approach to and interest in tasks, his reaction to failure, and his degree of perseveration. When used on successive occasions, they do provide some degree of qualified information, which is always better then casual unrelated observations.

A unique tool and a very useful one for nurses is the Functional Screening Tool devised by the University of Washington School of Nursing. This tool encompasses more behavior than the usual infant tests and developmental scales, but all items included are significant in the overall development of the child. The incorporation of such areas as feeding, sleeping, toilet-training, and play behavior makes it especially meaningful to nurses for these are the very areas in which we can be most instrumental in terms of intervention. Of equal importance to the developmental scale is the portion of the tool concerned with suggested activities. A review of nursing literature indicates that this accumulation of suggestions is one of the most complete and meaningful put together thus far.

Further evaluation of the scale is difficult without additional information, such as the normative sample used. The age intervals are long, considering the rapid development that occurs particularly in the first year. For example, a number of changes occur in the normally developing infant between the fourth and eighth month. Using the screening tool during this period, one can only make a rough estimate as to whether the child is functioning closer to the 4- or 8-month age level. It is also not clear if the items included in any single category, such as feeding, are in developmental sequence or whether two or three skills might be acquired simultaneously. For example, in the motor area, which apparently includes both fine and gross motor development, as well as some adaptive behavior, it is conceivable that three of six tasks might be acquired simultaneously at the 19-month level, but this would be sufficient to place his development halfway between the 19-to 30-months category: In this instance one does not know if the child is functioning at the 19- or 26-month level. On the other hand, this type of age spread does allow for individual differences in development as well as environmental influences, while at the same time establishing upper and lower limits for each skill. Perhaps our discussion period will allow us to explore the potential uses of this tool in more detail.

In addition to the more standardized methods of assessment, we have all seen publications in professional and lay journals presenting shortcut methods for assessing the development of the child. This has come about primarily because more conventional tests have been found to be impractical in some settings. Most test authors call for extensive training and experience or require the mastery of an accompanying manual as prerequisites for administering the test. In the face of more patients and less time, many doctors, nurses, and other professionals have turned to shortcuts, which can often be dangerous. To illustrate the preponderance of this situation, a recent survey in England revealed that 74 out of 132 doctors interviewed drew up their own tests, using a combination of items from published tests. In so doing, the standardization of any one test was invalidated, with the resultant score being meaningless except to give a rough estimate. In regard to short-cutting, it is well to remember that the fewer the items, the more unreliable the test.

While each of us may have confidence in our subjective ability to evaluate a child based on a few items, this can often be misleading. A study by Sam Kirk in 1960 illustrates this point.[18] In his study, he asked all pediatricians, social workers, public health nurses, and teachers in a community of 70,000 to refer all children between the ages of 3 and 5 who were functioning in the educable mentally retarded category. Physicians referred predominantly severely and moderately retarded children. The other professionals referred children who came from homes that were unsanitary or substandard. With those results, Dr. Kirk concluded that there was obviously a need for objective screening techniques.

The nurses in this study, as many of us here today, were guilty of basing estimates of children's functioning on intuition or a few milestones committed to memory. It is timely that we as nurses are today becoming more sophisticated in making developmental assessments of children and using the tools at our disposal.

It is no longer sufficient to describe a child's play activity or his self-help skills. It is necessary to make judgments about the appropriateness of play, degree of independence, and modes of adaptive functioning based on a scientific knowledge of growth and development and the objective measurement of behavior.

In addition to assessment of a child's developmental level in a screening sense, assessment tools can be useful to the nurse in a variety of other ways. Periodic assessments of a child's development can be utilized by the nurse in encouraging parents to provide an environment in which the demands placed upon the child are consistent with his abilities at each age. For example, a child who uses a palmar grip instead of a pincer grasp may have difficulty in buttoning or in performing other fine movements. Developmental assessments also provide the nurse with an index of the child's readiness for learning in regard to self-help skills. Areas of deficit can indicate areas to work with in home training. These tools can also be utilized to give valuable information about a child's personality and behavior. Draw-a-Man tests give clues to the child's self-concept. Test materials such as bells and pictures can give an estimate of vision or auditory ability. In metabolic diseases, such as PKU, hypothyroidism, and galactosemia, periodic evaluation of development may serve as a means of assessing the adequacy and results of treatment. The nurse through her home visits is in an excellent position to make periodic meaningful assessments and to add valuable developmental observations to the accumulating body of knowledge related to these disorders. In establishing operant conditioning programs, the nurse can make valuable base line observations about a child's functioning. As you can see, the possibilities are numerous.

A frequent theme in nursing discussions today is the need for improving levels of practice. The use of developmental assessment tools in appropriate situations will help those of us concerned with children to make more accurate judgments about the behavior we observe. If we are to use these tools, however, we must be taught. The question then is raised as to where the use of developmental testing can be most effectively taught. Are they to be taught in nursing schools, and if so, how, and at what level? Graduate students particularly might wish to acquire a more thorough knowledge of growth and development through the use of assessment tools. We who are working in the area of child development are interested in adding to our knowledge and skills. This undoubtedly holds true for nurses in hospitals, in institutions, in well-baby clinics, and in classrooms.

REFERENCES

1. Ames, L. B.: The constancy of psych-motor tempo in individual infants, J. Genet. Psychol. **57**:445-450, 1940.
2. Anastasi, A.: Psychological testing, ed. 2, New York, 1961, The Macmillan Co.
3. Anastasi, A.: Differential psychology, ed. 3, New York, 1962, The Macmillan Co.
4. Bayley, N.: Mental growth during the first three years, Genet. Psychol. Mongo. **14**:1-92, 1933.
5. Bayley, N.: Value and limitations of infant testing, Children **5**:129-134, July-Aug., 1958.
6. Mental measurements yearbook, 1965, Highland Park, N. J., 1965, Gryphon Press.
7. Caldwell, B., and Richmond, J.: The impact of theories of child development, Children **9**:73-78, March-April, 1962.
8. Cattell, P.: The measurement of intelligence of infants and young children, New York, 1940, Psychological Corp.
9. Doll, E.: The Vineland social maturity scale, Minneapolis, 1947, Educational Test Bureau.
10. Fischler, K., Graliker, B. V., and Koch, R.: The predictability of intelligence with Gesell developmental scales in mentally retarded infants and young children, Amer. J. Ment. Defic. **69**:515-525, 1965.
11. Freeman, F.: Theory and practice of psychological testing, New York, 1955, Henry Holt & Co.
12. Fromm, E., Hartman, L. D., and Marschak, M. A.: A contribution to a dynamic theory of intelligence testing of children, J. Clin. & Exper. Psychopath. **15**:73-95, 1954.
13. Gesell, A., and Amatruda, C. S.: Developmental diagnosis, ed. 2, New York, 1954, Paul Hoeber, Inc.
14. Gesell developmental testing (editorial), Pediatrics **30**:162-163, 1962.
15. Gibson, R.: Intellectual assessment of children, Develop. Med. Child Neurol., p. 510, 1964.

16. Hoffman, L. W., and Hoffman, M., editors: Review of child development research, vol. 2, New York, 1966, Russell Sage Foundation.
17. Illingworth, R. S.: The predictive value of developmental tests in the first year, with special reference to the diagnosis of mental subnormality, J. Child Psychol. Psychiat. **2:**210-215, 1961.
18. Kirk, S.: Early education of the mentally retarded, Urbana, Ill., 1958, University of Illinois Press.
19. Knobloch, H.: Developmental behavioral approach to neurologic examination in infancy, Child Develop. **33:**181, 1962.
20. Knobloch, H., and Pasamanick, B.: A developmental questionnaire for infants forty weeks of age, Monogr. Soc. Res. Child Develop. **20:**9-112, 1955.
21. Knobloch, H., and Pasamanick, B.: A developmental screening inventory for infants, part II, Pediatrics **38:**1095-1105, 1966.
22. Korsch, B., Cobb, K., and Ashe, B.: Pediatricians' appraisals of patients' intelligence, Pediatrics **27:**990-1003, 1961.
23. Matheny, A.: Improving diagnostic forecasts made on a developmental scale, Amer. J. Ment. Defic. **71:**371-375, 1966.
24. McFarland, J. W.: The uses and predictive limitations of intelligence tests in infants and young children, Bull. WHO **9:**409, 1953.
25. Mueller,: Mental testing in mental retardation: a review of recent research, Train. Sch. Bull. **60:**152, 1964.
26. Paine, R.: Neurologic examination of infants and children, Pediatric Clinics of North America, Philadelphia, August, 1960, W. B. Saunders Co.
27. Ruess, A., Trevino, L., Buzdygan, D., et al.: An experimental study of a pediatric screening test of the intelligence of pre-school children, Amer. J. Ment. Defic. **69:**506-513, 1965.
28. Silver, A.: Diagnostic value of three drawing tests for children, J. Pediat. **37:**129-143, 1950.
29. Thorpe, L.: Child psychology and development, New York, 1962, Ronald Press Co.

FOR ADDITIONAL INFORMATION

Developmental Screening Inventory
Division of Child Development
Ohio State University, College of Medicine
Columbus, Ohio

Vineland Social Maturity Scale
American Guidance Service, Inc.
Publisher's Building
Circle Pines, Minnesota 55014

Denver Developmental Screening Test
LADOCA Project and Publishing
Foundation, Inc.
51st Avenue and Lincoln Street
Denver, Colorado 80216

Goodenough-Harris Drawing Test
Harcourt Brace Jovanovich, Inc.
Test Department
757 Third Avenue
New York, New York 10017

INDEX